...AND GLADLY TEACH

THE ADVENTURE OF TEACHING

Other books in the MY LIFE AND MY WORK series:

'ONE OFF'   *by* T. E. Johnson
   The story of an advertising man

I SWEAR BY APOLLO   *by* P. T. Regester
   The life of a doctor

LIVING DIMENSIONS   *by* T. W. O. Carter
   The work of an architect

THE RING OF WORDS   *by* D. J. Hall
   An author writes of his work

CHILDREN IN JEOPARDY   *by* Joan Lawson
   The life of a Child Care Officer

THE DUSTLESS ROAD   *by* S. J. Harland
   A career in the Merchant Navy

CHEW THIS OVER   *by* Matthew Finch
   The life of a dentist

NEVER AT SEA   *by* Vonla McBride
   Life in the WRNS

Shortly to be published:

BOOKS ARE MY BUSINESS   *by* A. W. Reed
   The life of a publisher

CAN I HELP YOU MADAM?   *by* Marian Aitken
   Career opportunities in retailing

...AND
GLADLY TEACH

The Adventure of Teaching

BY

MARGARET MILES

with a Foreword by

SIR JOHN NEWSOM, C.B.E.

MY LIFE AND MY WORK SERIES

EDUCATIONAL EXPLORERS LIMITED
READING

Jacket design by
John Tomlinson

Published by Educational Explorers Limited
11 *Crown Street, Reading, England*
Set in '*Monotype' Bembo and printed in Great Britain by*
Lamport Gilbert & Co. Limited
Gun Street, Reading, England

CONTENTS

ACKNOWLEDGEMENT

For permission to publish the photographs in this
volume the Author and Publisher gratefully acknowledge
the help given by

The Bristol Education Authority
The Central Office of Information
The Marconi Company
also
Camera Press Limited
Henry Grant, Esq., A.I.I.P.
and
Thomson Newspapers Limited

ILLUSTRATIONS

Inset between pages 48 and 49

FOREWORD

By SIR JOHN NEWSOM, C.B.E.

THIS BOOK, which is the personal account of the education and experience of a distinguished Headmistress, is intended to inspire young people who are thinking about their future career.

It is a book which should not only inspire them and their parents, but be of interest to everyone concerned with Education; because it describes not only her personal experience but reflects changing attitudes towards many social and educational problems during the past thirty years. Changes in our ideas about the function of schools, the rôle of women in teaching and society as a whole; changes in the relationship between teachers and pupils and in the whole atmosphere of school staff rooms – changes which, for the most part, are for the better.

Through her eyes we see teaching in its setting today: a career which does not cut people off, but engages them vitally in the life of the community. For the young people to whom this book is addressed, it will be fascinating reading.

The book reflects Margaret Miles' compassion and belief in the individual, and it contains sound commentary on many of our current educational problems.

'. . . *and gladly would he learn and gladly teach*'

Prologue on the Clerk of Oxenford from

CHAUCER'S 'CANTERBURY TALES'

I

FACE TO FACE WITH CHILDREN

I DON'T KNOW how many there were, about forty, I suppose, but I do remember that I was frightened. It was a mixed class and the ages ranged from eleven to fourteen. They had little zest for learning and they were not very clever. They needed very special teaching and I was the last person who ought to have been coping with them. But there I was, my B.A. Hons. (History) London, still very new, my head full of all sorts of uneducational things, and my memories of the International Student Conference, from which I had just returned, still very vivid.

Why was I there? Well, as a student in receipt of a Board of Education grant I had to do three weeks' teaching practice in an elementary school. I was sent to Brandlehow Road School, Putney, an unreorganised elementary school whose ancient buildings were later destroyed by enemy action and on whose site now stands an attractive airy primary school from which we at Mayfield recruit annually a number of girls.

But when I went to Brandlehow it was mixed and all ages, and the headmaster, I believe not without malice, gave me his 'difficult' class. I had to teach them everything. I think it was the arithmetic I dreaded most, or was it the geography? I can still remember the long mornings and even more the long afternoons, the switching from subject to subject, the agonising discovery of how little I knew about the North and South Islands of New Zealand, and about how to communicate to my charges the common sense that lies at the heart of the decimal system.

I had not seriously thought about education at all. I still thought of teaching as the imparting of knowledge, but I quickly learnt that I had not got even the knowledge I expected them to want to have! I certainly had not thought about the processes of learning and how people communicate with each other. I just did not think of these boys and girls as human beings, growing up, trying to find things out for themselves. I thought of them simply as my raw material.

It took me a long time to realise that the art of teaching is to help people to learn, to find things out and to think for themselves. Too often in the classroom there is so much emphasis on knowledge that a barrier is built between the teacher and the taught, and adventurousness and inquisitiveness are lost.

Then, of course, we were preoccupied with what we were pleased to call discipline or order, and this order was imposed by the teacher on the children. I had not then thought of how a real educational order comes when people are engaged in doing things that they want to do and in which they are intensely interested.

My experience at Brandlehow made me see that teaching was something far more challenging and subtle than what I had done in Sunday School and in my childhood games.

My father was a Presbyterian Minister and on Sundays I used to go to church in the mornings and often in the evenings as well, and to Sunday School in the afternoons. I must have fancied myself as a preacher too, because at the age of nine or ten I used to line up my two young brothers and my sister, and any other docile members of the household who would play, and preach to them. I had had some pamphlets or tracts from Sunday School, one of which, I know, was on the evils of drink. These I used as the bases of my sermons. We sang hymns too.

In Sunday School it was usual, and I expect it still is, for the older girls and boys to take a group of small children during part of the service. We began all together for hymns, prayers and readings, and then broke up into groups for the story. This was my first experience of teaching. I must, I think, have been about twelve when I took my first Sunday School teacher's examination and I still have my first prize.

My mother who graduated at Aberystwyth where she met my father, taught for a few years at a girls' public day school, Trust High School; and then at one of the new secondary schools founded after the Education Act of 1902. When she married my father she gave up her job without question and became what we now call a 'wastage statistic'!

I was the second child and second daughter, and was born in Liverpool during a heat wave and a coal strike. After me came two boys. Although there are two years between us, I seem to remember that my sister and I both started school together; we went to a small private school with two teachers, and on the first day we were both asked, she first, to spell 'cat'. This was easy, I thought; just listen and say the same!

However, there must have been some educational ideas in the air at that school as I have a vivid memory of one of the teachers showing us how you could bend a poker when it was red hot. After a very short spell at school, my sister got mumps and I followed on. This kept us away from the pursuit of learning for quite a long time.

This was during the 1914-1918 war, and towards the end, after the zeppelins had been over London, we went to stay with our North Welsh grandmother, or *nain*, and attended the board school in Bala. It was the height of my ambition to be in standard six and go on errands for our class teacher, Miss Jones. I cannot remember anything of the lessons, but I know I began to write letters and was occasionally sent to buy things at the shop, so I suppose I could do some money sums.

We also spoke some Welsh and learnt by heart a lot of hymns and songs in Welsh and English. I was proud of this accomplishment and on our return to London insisted on singing the whole ten verses of *Bachcen Bach*, 'Little Child of Wales', in Welsh, at a children's party. I discovered later this was not at all popular, but at the time I was unaware of the consternation I caused. A bad mark for a future teacher, who should always be aware!

As this book is about teaching I shall go on to tell you a bit more about what I remember of my own experience of being taught. Schools and teachers have changed quite a lot since I was a pupil at school, but these very changes tell us much about the principles which underlie modern educational practice.

After a short spell at another small school, we moved to Felixstowe in Suffolk for my father's health. There a county secondary school for boys and girls had been established in a private house at the corner of our road. Although we were well under the age of eleven, my sister and I both attended. The school was later moved to an old manor house, a mile or so away along the bleak sea front, and we trudged to school there in all weathers.

It was a mixed school with a mixed staff and I think we were quite well taught in some subjects. I can remember only the silly and embarrassing incidents, as when I forgot where I was and called the scripture master 'Daddy' in class, and when I spilled paint water on my jersey. The teacher insisted on taking it off to get it dried and revealed to the whole class the shameful secret that my skirt was held up by boys' braces! This was one of my mother's practical ideas. We did learn some science and some maths, but nothing stands out except that I thought I liked algebra.

As well as my preaching activities I enjoyed 'reciting' at this stage and was very catholic in my taste. I remember that one of my 'turns' was the *Wreck of the Hesperus*. This I inflicted on the Ladies' Working Party and it was one of the very few occasions I ever remember when I forgot my lines! A mortifying experience. Later I became passionately fond of Keats' *La Belle Dame Sans Merci* and 'rendered' it on every possible occasion.

I think that this insistence on showing off was one of the traits in my character which made people think I should go in for teaching. In fact, although some histrionic ability is quite useful in the classroom, learning will not take place if the teacher relies on this alone.

I also read a great deal and particularly liked historical stories and adventure books. *Scott at the South Pole*, all of Henty's historical novels, Ballantyne and Stevenson widened my horizons and gave me a great deal of vicarious excitement. One of the books I read several times was *John Halifax, Gentleman*, and the one which I think moved me most deeply and which made me cry at the end was *The Cloister and the Hearth*. I must have picked up some history somewhere because I remember that I knew that the hero and heroine of Charles Read's book were the parents of Erasmus.

At eleven I went from Felixstowe to Ipswich High School where I got a free place through a war victim scholarship, and here my secondary education really began. I now consciously began to enjoy school; and, with others, ruthlessly assessed the skills of our teachers. We liked Miss X but she could not keep order, we disliked Miss Y who also could not, we did not like Miss Z but we did respect her and she could teach. However bad discipline or teaching was, we never thought of complaining about a member of staff and it has always come as a shock to me as a headmistress when girls have done so.

At our school we used to have lessons in the mornings only and private study, games and needlework in the afternoons. I developed a tremendous interest in games, and managed to go through all my seven years at Ipswich without ever going to needlework. I had no opportunity to do cookery, which I regret, but we took art throughout the whole course and music, though this did not rank high in our estimation.

I have often wished I had been better educated musically. We had singing in the hall once a week with a visiting teacher, but we used to fool about and did not take it seriously. What I did learn musically was from my piano teacher (we nearly all had piano lessons) and the mother of one of my friends, who had me to stay and who used to play for us and her two brothers while we attempted duets and part songs.

The years spent at secondary school are years in which we change enormously. It is at secondary school that the frontiers of childhood are crossed, but I know that I remained very unsophisticated throughout my school days; at least, socially and emotionally, though perhaps less so intellectually. Although I would certainly not claim that my schooldays were the happiest days of my life, I did enjoy them. I liked the work and, except for one rebellious year, did more than enough homework.

I loved English because I liked reading and acting, and in the sixth began to appreciate French and eventually Latin. Mathematics and science I coped with but never warmed to and in those days it was unusual to do science unless one was very good at it. Although I liked reading historical novels and biographies I did not think of history (in which I later took my degree) as my 'best' subject.

We had no outside school activities in the modern sense such as youth clubs, swimming clubs and orchestras. The school claimed our total loyalty. The Guide company was a school company and the same girls who played games together in school went to Guide camp in the holidays. I loved camping, and still do, but in the Sixth I decided I was against Guides. I have since swung back to realising what a good Guide company or some similar organised group can do for young people. I have also come to admire very much those teachers who, in addition to their normal teaching duties, undertake extra things like camps and school journeys. We did not have school journeys as such although I do remember that there was an expedition to Giggleswick to see the eclipse. It was expensive and I did not go; but it must have been quite an undertaking. What travel abroad I had was organised by my parents and not by the school.

The first adventure was a trip to Belgium in a cargo steamer whose captain was known to my father. I think he had done Captain Blonde some service and in return the captain invited him to take his two daughters across the North Sea in his ship.

We set off from Felixstowe dock in bright sunshine, but it was fairly rough and I was very sick, and by the time we arrived at Nieuport I was pretty miserable. Our brief visits to Brussels and to Middleburgh were overcast by the dread of the return journey. Actually it was calm and still; it was at night and a great thrill.

A few years later I went to France to spend three weeks of the Easter holiday with an old friend of my mother's. Mme. Metge had been a teacher in the Lycée, where my mother had spent a year as what we now call an *Assistante* before she began teaching, and she and her husband lived in a large grey house called *Chantemerle* in Lèves near Chartres.

I learnt quite a lot of French and studied Racine hard, but I did not have an exciting time. I cannot remember meeting any young people at all and I was certainly a little homesick and often bored. No girl of seventeen today would accept being 'done good to' so passively, I am sure, but it never occurred to me to complain or carp. I just thought I was lucky being allowed to be in France, and I did get to know Chartres Cathedral very well. It was the one expedition I was permitted and I made it frequently.

This dependence on our parents is one of the things which differentiates my generation from corresponding young people today. It was basically a financial dependence for we had no opportunities to earn money by working in shops or hotels or camps. There was no casual work because there were armies of unemployed waiting for any jobs that were going, and in any case it would not have been considered socially acceptable. Decisions about university or other higher education were also made more by the parents than by the school.

It had always been assumed at home that I would go to the university. From Ipswich people usually went to Cambridge and if I had stayed on at Ipswich until I left school I might have gone to Girton as did Peggy S—— my contemporary and rival up the school. She was cleverer than I was and I am afraid she worked much harder too. For a long time I kept a notebook of humorous verse she wrote on all sorts of school situations. However, at the end of my lower sixth year, my parents moved to Surrey and though I stayed for one more year at Ipswich to take higher certificate I moved to Croydon High School for my third year in the sixth.

At Croydon the tradition was for girls to go to Oxford and I joined a group who were going to take their university entrance that year; at the same time we worked for our London higher certificate in four subjects with a view to getting exemption from London intermediate if we should in the end go to a London College. Because I liked reading and acting, I had always assumed that I would take my university entrance in English and no one had tried to dissuade me.

It was at Croydon that I realised that English was not for me. My moment of truth came in an English lesson, when I was asked to criticise Wordsworth's short poem,

> '*A slumber did my spirit seal,*
> *I had no human fears,*
> *I seemed a thing that did not feel*
> *The touch of earthly years.*'

I was struck dumb; the words were meaningless. I was an ignorant stupid thing with no spirit at all and just blushed and mumbled.

Humiliated and ashamed I decided to give up English and

Oxford; I asked the history mistress whether she thought I could do enough English history to do the Bedford College entrance exam which was not far ahead. She did not really know me, but she was not discouraging, so that is what I did. I have never been sorry that I changed to history though I have from time to time regretted not having gone to Oxford.

I should perhaps say a word about money here, because actually it would have been difficult financially for me to have gone to Oxford. There were no 'life size' grants in those days and county and state scholarships were grants towards the cost and were not intended to cover expenses, which were considered the responsibility of parents. Many schools gave small scholarships and grants of something like £20 to £30 and of course there were the open scholarships, (also small for girls), as now.

Most schools and some local authorities had loan funds and many young graduates started their teaching career with a load of debt which, though honourable, was very heavy. Another method of paying one's way was through the Board of Education four-year grant for those who were going to teach. This was known as the 'pledge' because those who accepted it, and I was one, had to undertake to teach at the end of their course. The fourth year was, of course, to be spent in a university department of education.

Though I hated the idea of tying myself to teaching through the pledge, this is what I had to do. It took me to Bedford College for three years and then for one year to the London University Institute of Education which was the new name just adopted by the former London Day Training College, housed in the building in Southampton Row which is now the Central School of Arts and Crafts.

My three weeks' teaching practice at Brandlehow Road happened between finishing at Bedford College and beginning at the Institute. It was through my experience then that I began to learn that the authority of a teacher does not come automatically and that it will not come at all unless the needs of the learner are understood. My childhood ideas of playing school had been very much teacher centred and authoritarian. The real thing, as I encountered it, was very different; and nowadays is very different again.

Today classrooms are more like workrooms; that is to say that they are learning rooms rather than teaching rooms. When I began I was obsessed with teaching and of course I was not a success. In clearing out old papers I have come across my teaching notebook for Brandlehow Road; it is a historical document if only in the sense that it is very old fashioned. For one thing the emphasis is strongly on content rather than method. I tried to teach about verbs and adverbs, nouns and adjectives, I tried to teach about decimals, fractions and money sums, I tried to teach about King Arthur, about the North and South Islands of New Zealand, and in almost every case I was resisted and the class just did not learn!

The notes that I made after my supervisor had come tell me that I looked too grim and that I did not manage to make the class do the work. More than once I noted the difficulty I found in seeing that everybody was working, and I recorded my admiration of the teachers who seemed to have achieved this objective.

I remember that I was taken off my first difficult class. They had made rings round me! The boys kept asking to be excused and I dared not refuse them. Then one day the door opened and Bill, one of the worst, was led back by the ear by the headmaster.

I was told in front of the class that I must not let these boys do what they liked, that they always tried it on with the new young teachers, and that I must be firmer with them. The result of all this was that I often felt that teaching was not for me.

Oddly enough, while I was doing my teaching practice I stayed with an old college friend of my mother's who was teaching at Putney County Secondary School, known as Mayfield. Little did I think then that years later I would become Head of Putney County School and would be Head at the time when it was converted from a selective grammar school into a comprehensive school.

2

A STUDENT IN TRAINING

I WENT UP to Bedford College then as an intending teacher. Many, but by no means all of my contemporaries, were going to teach. Those of us who were, thought rather more of teaching our subjects than of teaching children. This is not surprising as we had all been taught by subject specialists in our secondary schools, and we were engaged on an academic course and not a professional one.

My first year at Bedford was an interrupted and unorthodox one because, just after leaving school in July, I developed a virulent ear infection after doing too much diving and underwater swimming. This involved me in a double mastoid operation followed by pneumonia and general septicaemia. It was all very unpleasant and, as it was before the days of antibiotics, I had to struggle through without the chemical aids which now reduce temperatures and combat infection.

Because of all this I was not able to present myself at Bedford at the beginning of the Autumn Term and did not go up until November. Mercifully I had passed my four higher certificate subjects and was exempted from intermediate, the first part of the B.A. degree examination which was usually taken at the end of the first year.

At this time I very much wanted to read sociology and not

history, and I did actually attend lectures in the sociology department for a time, but my task masters at the Institute disapproved because they said that it was not a teaching subject. So I changed back to history and chose economic history as my special subject and the economic and social history of the Tudors as my special period. For this latter course we went to Professor Tawney and Professor Eileen Power at the London School of Economics.

Professor Penson, who later became Dame Lilian Penson and held office as Vice-Chancellor, had just taken over the history department at Bedford. I remember being very much impressed by her tendency to travel in taxis (which I still feel to be rather wickedly extravagant), and I much enjoyed her lectures on modern history.

I am afraid I did not work very hard and I remember being somewhat overawed by so many fellow students who did. I did not spend as much time on playing games as I had done at school, and I was one of the few of my year who did no boating.

At that time nearly all first year students boated on the lake in Regent's Park. You started in a 'tub' which held two oarswomen and a cox (earlier generations had had a chaperone as well!) and graduated to much more elegant craft with sliding seats. But by the time I arrived at College all my contemporaries were well ahead and I did not attempt to catch up. I played tennis in the summer term instead.

It was while I was at Bedford that I began to learn about committee procedures. We were all automatically members of the Students' Union and I was among those who used to attend most of the meetings. We had a debating society too and I think this gave me my first experience of formal debating. I remember too that we had a mock election and anticipated the defeat of the Labour government.

Towards the end of my second year I was invited to stand for election as President of the Students' Union. I do not remember the election campaign very well, nor how the votes were cast, but I was elected and in my third and final year presided over the Union Committee meetings and the general meetings.

Domestic business seemed to go fairly smoothly except for the affair of the college colours. Before 1914 these had been black, yellow and red, but during the war of 1914-18 a patriotic group of students had decided that it was disloyal to wear them as they were the German national colours. So the College colours were changed to green and silver. When I was president there was a move to change back and a referendum was held. Some form of proportional representation was used in the voting as there were three choices. In the end I think the *status quo* won.

It all sounds rather a storm in a tea-cup now, but I remember at the time there was some very strong feeling and the whole exercise was a very interesting lesson in the extremely complicated process of testing public opinion.

In my day the Bedford Union did not have much to do with U.L.U. (this was before they had the splended buildings in Malet Street) but we were active in N.U.S. and I was privileged to be elected a Vice-President. In this capacity I attended executive and council meetings at N.U.S. headquarters and up and down the country.

I remember Bristol, Manchester, Liverpool, Sheffield and Birmingham very well, and there were possibly others. I found these visits most interesting and they certainly opened my eyes to the vitality of the great civic universities, of which I had previously been completely unaware, as indeed, I think, were many of my contemporaries at Bedford.

N.U.S. had its international associations and was a member of the *Conféderation Internationale des Etudiants*, an international student body which had been formed after the first World War. It was, as was the League of Nations, European centred and was dominated by the French and British.

I was lucky enough to be sent as a delegate to the Annual Congress at Riga, then the capital of a small independent Baltic republic. We were routed through Czechoslovakia where we attended the Conference of International Student Service at Brno. From Brno we travelled by train northwards through Poland to Riga. We had an hour or so in Warsaw and the one thing I remember vividly was the groups of beggars on the steps of the churches. I think we changed at Warsaw into a wide gauge Russian type of rolling stock.

In Riga we were constantly reminded of the Latvian struggle against the Germans in the '14-'18 War and could not but admire the Latvians' gallant attempts at establishing a democratic republic. The same pattern was to be seen in Lithuania, Esthonia and Finland. All had new constitutions and wonderful Parliament Houses with facilities some of which are still lacking in the Palace of Westminster.

Soviet Russia was not far away geographically, but as I remember was rarely discussed and was emotionally a distant and different world. The Times correspondent for Russian affairs wrote from Riga and there seemed to be a little daily contact with Russia itself.

The students, who all wore the peaked caps of the Scandinavian and German student, were keenly nationalist and when we suggested a Baltic federation, dismissed it because of language and national differences. Now all three countries are states of the Soviet Union.

I do not remember the student business we discussed but I do remember the anxiety of the Hungarians to get us to discuss Treaty Revision, and the persistent refusal of some members to pay their subscriptions.

The leader of our delegation was the President of the Union of Nottingham University; he is now Secretary of the Football Association. He was a sturdy leader and delightful companion. He taught me to dance a quick waltz and we became very good at it, particularly the reverse step.

The following year C.I.E. met in Venice and then I went on to Turin with the British Women's Tennis Team for the International Student Games. I did not enjoy this first trip to Italy; for one thing I developed a temperature and sore throat in Venice and was very miserable. But the real horror was the way the Fascists were beginning to dominate everything.

The parade of the teams was quite overshadowed by Fascist military displays; every bit of applause turned into *Duce! Duce! Duce!* thundered rhythmically by the crowds. The whole atmosphere was hostile and menacing. I managed to get to Rome on a private visit and can remember the frighteningly brilliant presentation of a sort of exhibition-chapel-memorial to the martyrs of the Fascist revolution when Mussolini had marched to Rome. It was all there, soft lights, music, and I believe even recorded voices; insidious, false, but very clever. I was very glad to be able to go back to Rome more recently with a group organised by the Council for Education in World Citizenship. This time I loved it and long to go again.

My Baltic journey took place just before I began my teaching practice at Brandlehow Road and was not altogether a good preparation for it!

During the three weeks at Brandlehow I went on a visit to Croydon High School where I was to do my secondary school teaching practice. This was to go on all through the training year, but not in blocks as it is now done. We used to go to the school for two days a week and be at the Institute of Education for the remaining three.

I had no choice as to whether I should take a year of professional training because my undertaking to the Board of Education committed me to doing so. There are, however, still some people who say that teacher training is unnecessary, that good natural teachers do not need to train, and they quote famous headmasters who have reached the top of their profession as examples of those who do well without training.

This attitude, to my mind, is complacent and unimaginative and insulting to the profession. It endorses the slur summarised in the slogan 'those who can, do; those who can't, teach; those who can't teach, teach teachers', and so on, and it gives support to the heresy that the most important part of teaching is the imparting of knowledge.

The value of the year of professional training following a degree course at a university is very considerable, although it is not always obvious at the time. One positive advantage is that the student is a year older when she faces her first professional job, and that year has been spent very largely in studying the background and history of education and educational institutions, and acquiring an elementary knowledge of psychology.

The student in training also has an opportunity to observe

teachers, some good, some bad; and to be observed while herself teaching. It also limits the effects of her mistakes. I remember at the time I did not enjoy or appreciate my training year, particularly the theoretical side, but looking back I am convinced that it was valuable.

To have to stop and think, to have to reorientate oneself after the rather intensive academic study for an honours degree, to have to think of the details of school organisation, of classroom activity, of how children behave, is good. I would never agree that we should continue the old pattern of assuming that a degree qualifies anybody to be a teacher. I hope it will not be long before professional training is compulsory for all teachers in all schools maintained by Local Education Authorities.

3

WHAT KIND OF TEACHER?

BRANDLEHOW ROAD SCHOOL was an all-age elementary school. Most of the children came to it at the age of five and stayed until fourteen. Between nine and thirteen some of the cleverer children or those of more ambitious parents, 'passed the scholarship' and got a free place in the local secondary school; some others went off to trade schools where they could get an education up to fifteen or sixteen with a vocational bias towards the clothing trade or commerce or building or cookery. The rest stayed in their elementary school.

It was the Act of 1944 which turned all the schools for children over the age of eleven in England and Wales into secondary schools. At the same time fees were abolished in all secondary schools. In this way the former elementary schools were given a new status by being financially administered on the same terms as were the well-established grammar schools. The school leaving age was officially raised from fourteen to sixteen; although it was immediately possible to raise it only to fifteen. In 1964 the Government accepted the recommendation in the Newsom Report that it should be raised to sixteen in 1970.

But not only have there been changes in the reorganisation of schools, there have been enormous changes in the training and in the attitudes of teachers. The teachers of the three classes which I was allowed to teach at Brandlehow Road had probably been to a teacher training college (now Colleges of Education) for two years, and they were qualified to teach in elementary schools but not in secondary schools.

Incidentally on the whole it was correct to call the elementary school teachers 'assistant teachers', but the secondary school teachers 'assistant masters' or 'assistant mistresses'. The assistant mistresses that I saw at the Croydon High School, when I went to discuss my teaching practice, were all university graduates and they were mostly specialists in one subject which they taught all the time.

I cannot help feeling it is regrettable that this tendency to use specialist teachers has now spread to the schools that used to be the elementary schools, so that more and more people want to teach a subject to a lot of children rather than a lot of things to fewer children.

Another change is the coming together of the two kinds of teacher. Now, those who teach in secondary grammar schools do not mind being called teachers. Today also all the teachers who have been to teacher training colleges must have been there for at least three years—another reform which was brought in in 1963.

There is still a distinct difference between the two kinds of preparation for being a teacher, though the teachers from the Colleges of Education and those from the universities are coming closer together. A student at a College of Education continues her own personal education and at the same time studies the theory and practice of teaching. This involves commitment to the job of teaching before even beginning a college course.

A university student on the other hand continues her personal education for three years and then takes a degree in the subject in which she has specialised and is still theoretically free to choose a profession other than teaching. If, however, she does want to go on to teaching she concentrates her professional, vocational training for teaching in one year either in a University Department of Education or at a College of Education.

In the staff-room of any large school, at various times of the school year, will be found several young men or women who look rather more anxious than those younger members of the staff, who perhaps became fully fledged teachers only a few months before. These will be the students. If the school is a large secondary school catering for all ranges of ability there will be some students from Colleges of Education and some students from University Departments of Education.

What they are all there for is to do the practical part of their training known as 'teaching practice'. The amount of actual teaching that is done will vary according to the college or institution that the student belongs to, as will also the amount of supervision. In some cases most of the supervision may well be in the hands of the teaching staff of the school, in others it will be done more by visiting lecturers from the colleges.

The training of education students through teaching practice is a part of teaching which is of immense interest. It is one of the ways in which the profession does help itself and tries to raise its own standards and perpetuate the best in its traditions. There is, of course, a danger of old methods being passed on without question, but this is on the whole counteracted by the bringing of new experimental ideas into the schools through the conferences with the training institutions and by the students themselves.

Until I reached the sixth form I had always wanted to teach but as far as I remember I had not been very specific about what sort of a teacher I wanted to be. I suppose in a vague sort of way I thought I would like to be like the nicer ones of those who taught me. In the sixth I decided, however, that that was the last thing I wanted to be, and I had vague visions of myself as a doctor or doing social work or trying to do something international.

I set myself against teaching and resisted my headmistress's advice that I should apply for the four-year grant. In the end I gave in, with bad grace I'm afraid, secretly hoping that I would not stay in teaching very long. My three-year degree course and fourth year of professional training determined that I should become a history teacher in a secondary grammar school.

But what other sorts of teacher might I have been? Or perhaps that is a silly question because this book is written from my point of view, so perhaps we should ask what other sorts of teachers did some of my friends become?

Well, there was Natalie who went to the Froebel Educational Institute to take a three-year course of personal education and teacher training based on Froebelian methods. Then there was Joyce who went to a college of physical education where she specialised in games and gymnastics, took some additional training in first-aid and medical gymnastics and was prepared to go into school as a full-time physical education specialist. There were others who went to domestic science training colleges at Gloucester and Edinburgh, and these took three-year courses in the teaching of domestic subjects and also continued their own education.

But the great majority of teachers went to general teacher

training colleges where they had a two-year course in the theory and practice of education which qualified them to teach in the elementary schools. There the curriculum was simple and traditional: it did not include French, or anything more than the most elementary science usually called nature study and not practised in a laboratory. There was arithmetic rather than mathematics, drill rather than games, dance and gymnastics, and the teacher's main function was to see that the children from the elementary schools went out well versed in the three R's.

Until 1945 the salary structure of the teachers in the elementary schools was quite separate from that of those, mostly graduates, in the secondary schools. But the act of 1944 which established the principle of secondary education for all was followed by a rearrangement of the Burnham salary award so that all teachers got a basic scale, whatever kind of school they were teaching in.

This was calculated according to their own experience and training. On top of the basic scale, certain allowances were given for degrees, higher degrees, postgraduate training, and so on.

At last the foundations were laid for a teaching profession which could be mobile across the whole secondary field. During the years since 1944 there has been a tremendous development of the curriculum and attitudes in the modern secondary schools which have grown out of the old senior elementary schools. This development has given greatly increased scope and opportunity to teachers and, of course, to the Colleges of Education; it is increasing its pace all the time and the recommendation of the Robbins Committee, which envisaged a further great expansion both of the aims and of the content of teacher training, is increasing still more the rate of change.

Now, somebody who goes to a College of Education and takes

a concurrent course leading to a Certificate of Education is qualified to teach, and is able to teach, in any kind of secondary school including those previously staffed almost entirely by graduates. Certain Colleges of Education now give degrees in education, B.Ed., as well as Teachers' Certificates.

The great majority of students in the Colleges of Education are being trained for junior or infant school teaching. There is now a bridge course, called the junior secondary course, and this is very valuable to the student as it gives her great flexibility in the choice of posts when she leaves the college. It enables the colleges also to be more flexible in the teaching experience the students have and in the approach to the curriculum subjects, that is, the subjects the students are learning to teach.

Of course, another advantage for the secondary schools is that the junior secondary training does not aim to produce specialists; and a young teacher coming into a secondary school with a junior secondary training can well develop into one of these most valuable form mistresses or tutors who gets to know the children in her care well, in fact who is a teacher of children and not a teacher of a subject.

But there are still the two extreme ends of a young person's education that we have not yet dealt with. There is nursery school teaching and nursery nursing, and this is a field of education which is developing very much. Students can do nursery teaching after the normal course of teacher training, and nursery nursing by training in a day or residential children's nursery and taking the examinations of the N.N.E.B. The nursery and infant schools are staffed entirely by women, but primary and secondary schools may be staffed either by men or women.

Another field which seems to appeal particularly to women is teaching physically or mentally handicapped children in Special Schools. This work usually demands specialist training beyond the general teacher's course as well as unusual personal qualities.

At the other end of the spectrum there is university teaching, and I remember one of my contemporaries who got a scholarship to Girton (the one who worked harder and was cleverer than I); she was the sort of person who could have stayed at university to do research and perhaps, after taking a higher degree, become a university teacher. There is now an enormous expansion of all the university institutions and a great demand for more and more university teaching, but here necessarily the main emphasis is more on the actual academic qualifications of the candidate for the job than on his or her qualities as a person suitable for teaching.

The university teacher seems much freer than the teacher in school. She gives far fewer lectures than the school teacher gives lessons, she does not have to appear at college at half-past eight or nine in the morning, every morning, she does not have to take her form to assembly, or to do dinner duty and she has longer holidays than the school teacher has.

It must always be remembered, though, that universities are not only places for teaching undergraduates, they are places where research is done and where the frontiers of knowledge are pushed further and further outwards. The university teacher has to do original work, as well as teach undergraduates.

Mention must also be made of the Colleges of Education, which usually recruit their staffs from among serving teachers. They too offer splendid career opportunities and much interesting work.

4

ON BEING AN ASSISTANT MISTRESS

TEACHING HAD ALWAYS been thought of as an honourable profession in my family. It was approved because it was a safer and more suitable profession for girls than others were then thought to be; and also in the Welsh and Nonconformist milieu from which I came it was respected for what it was. But in the thirties there were more teachers than jobs and many were unemployed. We were all expendable.

Nowadays we do not know how we are going to get enough teachers to staff the schools over the next twenty years, but only thirty years ago there seemed to be too many. This, of course, is due to vast economic changes, but is also the result of a change in the general attitude to education. Then we gave most children as little education as possible and now we give them as much as possible.

It was tough looking for a teaching post in the thirties and, as the training year wore on, the main topic of conversation at the Institute came to be when and where we would get jobs. We had testimonials printed as we pored over the advertisement pages of the educational press. We were prepared to go anywhere. Most of our applications produced no response at all, and older headmistress colleagues have told me how they used then to have hundreds of applications for every advertised post.

I was interviewed for a few posts, but by the end of my training year neither I nor most of my contemporaries had got jobs. I was lucky then to be told of a possible vacancy at Westcliff High School where the head had been formerly on the staff of Ipswich High School. This was not to be filled until the following spring term, but I decided that if I could find something to do for the next six months I should be very lucky to be considered for this post.

It was then that I heard of the post of English teacher in the Töchter Institut at Klosters in Switzerland. This was a small finishing school run by a German Swiss schoolmaster and his wife for an international *clientèle* which very rarely included any English girls. I wrote; and was offered the post.

At last I was going to earn something, but I had to pay my own fare out. I went to Germany on my way to Switzerland and stayed with a family near Berlin. The father was Jewish and he was just beginning to feel the threat of Nazi persecution. Indeed that summer of 1934 was probably the last in which they were able to treat Dr. Goebbels as a joke.

From Berlin I went to Nuremberg and stayed with a family there. The father was a lawyer, a liberal one, and he was against the Nazis. I never heard what happened to him when the war came. During the time that I was in Germany I managed to pick up a bit of German and when I arrived at the Töchter Institut I was not quite helpless. Switzerland was fun and I learnt to ski.

In February I returned to England to be interviewed for the job at Westcliff High School, which I mercifully got.

I felt very proud to be beginning my first job. Although I had received some payment for my teaching in Switzerland it was little more than pocket money. Nowadays there can be few young teachers starting work at 22 years of age who have never actually earned any money regularly before, but when I began it was exceptional to have done so.

My first cheque therefore made me feel rich and independent. It was in fact very small and I think my annual salary was £217. I lived in a bed-sitter in a bungalow and had breakfast and an evening meal supplied, but I cannot remember how much I paid. I walked or bicycled to school, and always wore a hat, gloves, and, of course, stockings—not nylons because they did not exist.

I cannot remember the details of my first day. It was in May and it was one of those fine springs with blue skies and strong east winds. It was the year, too, of the silver jubilee of King George and Queen Mary and I remember getting a lift with one of my new colleagues to go up to London very early on a Sunday morning; I think it was to see the rehearsal for the procession.

As for what happened in school I find it very difficult to recall my first lessons or my first staff meeting or my first encounter with what was then a Board of Education register. I know I was not entirely free of discipline problems and I can remember the forms which gave me my most unhappy times.

Of course, they were trying me out and they certainly managed to get the better of me. I cannot remember whether it took a complete year for me to get over these difficulties and to gain confidence; not complete confidence, but enough confidence to be comfortable and to look forward to my lessons with cheerful anticipation and not with anxious dread.

The school was a four-stream Local Education Authority secondary school (grammar) in a fairly new building in a developing part of Westcliff. About half the children had free places, and parents then paid small fees for the others. The school was fairly rigidly streamed according to ability, or rather according to termly examination results, and each year was arranged in four forms, e.g. 1A1, 1A2, 1B1, 1B2.

2B2 were my special care for my first term and I taught them a lot, that is to say I taught them for a great deal of time! Whether they learnt anything I am not sure, but I had to teach them history, English, scripture and games so I met them once or twice every day. They had a way of diverting the course of the lesson which I had carefully planned. Had I been more experienced I would have been able to make use of the byways that they opened up, but I was still anxious to teach them in the way I had prepared and became more and more frustrated when I found I could not carry out the plan for my lesson.

I suppose the art of teaching is to make the pupils want to do what the teacher wants them to want to do—in other words, to create a situation, an atmosphere, in which learning can take place.

The first failures are very depressing, but the first awareness that something is happening is immensely exciting. I can re-member a first-form history lesson on Greece when the class and I took a leap forward, and their response gave new dimensions to my own thinking. Oddly enough it began with some simple ploy like the discussion of words used in the modern world which derived from the Greek language, but it led to a whole lot of considerations and to an imaginative exploration into the life and times of a Greek boy.

Indeed there is nothing like teaching for making one learn; and I certainly remember more and understand better those bits of history and literature that I tried to teach than those I was taught. I even became quite attached to 2B2 in the end because we did learn quite a lot together.

I remember too some sixth form lessons when the experience of having to expound a topic began a whole train of questioning of my own assumptions. There is no doubt that a sixth form group that is prepared to think and not just acquire facts for reproduction in an examination paper can be a most rewarding experience for any teacher.

I had always been keen on games and was anxious to help with teaching games, but I did not enjoy doing so. This was another revelation to me; I had always thought that most people liked games and it was only when I began to teach hockey that I realised that the majority of girls did not want to play hockey and did not like it when they had to. At last it is now being generally recognised that hockey is not the ideal form of exercise for all girls.

I was at Westcliff for nearly five years. I worked hard, but I lived in a fairly carefree way. I read a lot, and I think it was then that I read Macaulay's *History of England* with much enjoyment. I played tennis at the local club, I went to dances, and I went to London to the theatre. I went home for half term or any special week-ends. I was interested in the League of Nations Union, and helped with the Nansen pioneer camps in Devon during the holidays.

My proudest possession was a second-hand Baby Austin, the 'pram' type, which I bought for £25 and drove recklessly and often, I regret to say, brakelessly, to all sorts of places. I could not really afford it and I suppose I should have saved my money, but it gave me a great deal of fun and a sense of adventure.

It is in these first years of teaching that you really lay the foundation of your professional skill, and I think that anybody who has taught in her early twenties for two or more years would always be able to come back into a school even though methods and attitudes change. She will have acquired the indefinable something which establishes a relationship between the teacher and the pupils, a relationship which at its best can provide the background for real adventures in learning.

Teaching is certainly one of those professions which is very suitable for married women, who inevitably have to give up work during the time when their children are young, but who may well want to take up a professional job again when their children are of school age. With short courses on method, and content certainly in some subjects, a middle-aged woman who has taught for a year or two can much more easily adapt herself to school life than one who remembers school only from the point of view of being a pupil.

It is heartening that many people are coming back into teaching in middle age; and the fact that they are should encourage girls, who know they are going to marry fairly young, to undertake a training for teaching and to practise it for at least two years before they withdraw from it and concentrate on their homes and families.

Teachers have a twofold duty; they teach their subject or subjects to a lot of children throughout the school and they usually have a form or tutor group to look after as well. Part of the art of teaching is the establishment of the right relationship, whether teaching or pastoral, with the group so that its members are helped to be in a good relationship to other people as well.

A good form mistress must not get into that exclusive and

special relationship with her form which makes them eat out of her hand and do anything for her, but puts them at odds with everybody else. How often have I heard in the staff-room, when complaints have been made about a certain group, the injured and possessive form mistress saying 'I can't understand it, they're perfectly all right with me' (or 'for me' I think is usually the term used).

In her novel *The Prime of Miss Jean Brodie*, Muriel Spark tells of a teacher whose form throughout the school were 'holy terrors' in the eyes of everybody else, but were her special pets the *crème de la crème*, of whom she was inordinately proud and over whom she wielded a very considerable power. It is, I think, a sign of immaturity in a teacher to try to establish, and to succeed in establishing, this kind of relationship.

The only proper relationship between a form mistress or form tutor and her charges is one that is going to help them to gain independence and a standard of behaviour which is going to put them in an equally good relationship with everybody else. Indeed the more I see of teaching and of schools the more I realise that the whole process of education is concerned with creating an elaborate pattern of relationships.

At Westcliff I had certain extra-curricular jobs to do and I was put in charge of organising sideshows for the sports day. I am not very clever at this kind of thing, but I know I devised fishing rods with curtain rings on the end which had to drop over the necks of bottles. Athletics were not taken as seriously as they are nowadays, but the sports day was a very pleasant occasion when parents and pupils and staff were all together on the school premises enjoying outdoor recreations in a different sort of way from an ordinary teaching day.

Another of the jobs that I was given to do was to organise debates between the sixth forms of the girls' school and the Westcliff High School for Boys which was next door and whose grounds marched with ours. This was a fairly revolutionary activity as the boys and girls hardly met at all and the two schools had different starting and finishing hours of the school day so that boys and girls should not accompany each other home. The debates were quite formal but we did manage to get quite a fair proportion of the representatives of each school taking an active part.

I also very much enjoyed acting and producing plays and we had a certain amount of drama at Westcliff. Occasionally a play was put on for a house function. I do not think we had house drama competitions as such, or festivals, but I do remember taking part in the staff house play, and also in a school play. It was decided to produce *St. Joan* by Shaw, but as there were so many men's parts the producer asked if I might be given permission to take the part of the Inquisitor, which had the advantage that it could be separated off from the play more easily than any other part.

This I enjoyed doing very much, although in my heart of hearts I would really have liked to take the part of Joan. I had always had to take men's parts at school and secretly longed to be able to play a women's part. I think the only time I ever did so was in a staff play at Badminton when we did *The Late Christopher Bean* and I was allowed to be Gwenny the maid, because of my Welsh ancestry and my consequent familiarity with a Welsh accent. Both at school and college all the plays I acted in had all-female casts, which seems odd today.

As I look back on my years at Westcliff I can see that it was there that I truly served an apprenticeship. I learnt the craft of teaching and it was a tough and a sound apprenticeship.

I was lucky to begin in a well organised if formal school and to be thrown in at the deep end by having to cope with pretty large numbers and a great amount of preparation and of marking. Although I was promoted to be head of the history department and a housemistress at Westcliff it was in my next post that I learnt more of the philosophy of education and became more aware of its wider issues.

The advertisement for the post at Badminton School appeared early in the school year 1938/9, but I did not apply for it, although various friends had pointed it out to me, until the closing date was practically on me, if not already past. The reputation of the school in international and League of Nations Union circles stood very high and it was from these sources that I was pressed in the end to put in an application.

I went to the interview in a rather shabby tweed coat and resisted the pressure to borrow something smarter from my colleagues. My judgement was right: Badminton did not approve of fur coats. I was offered the post but did not feel one hundred per cent sure that I wanted to work in a girls' independent boarding school. In fact I felt very depressed as I went back to London. But I never regretted my decision to accept the post. I owe the school a great deal and I became a keen Badmintonian.

This was in March 1939 and by the time I eventually went to Badminton in Bristol, war had broken out. It was typical of the school that two members of staff, both of whom were later to become my personal friends, were unable to be present at the beginning of the Autumn term because they had been detained in Scandinavia, as they had gone to Russia for their summer holidays and had been caught by the outbreak of war.

Badminton was, and is, a progressive school with a strong international outlook and the time-table and curriculum were altogether freer than what I had been used to at Westcliff. It was also, of course, a very much smaller school (the teaching groups too were smaller) and included girls of a fairly wide range of ability. Terms were shorter but the working day and working week were necessarily longer. We did not have to do long domestic duties and had to take only a very modest share in general supervision.

The school was divided into houses and it was from their house base that the girls went out to their teaching groups. The housemistress had the pastoral and social care of the girls, but everybody knew everybody else whether in her house or other people's houses because of the smallness of the school. This was a very different kind of experience from my first post, but was a very enriching one.

I had to do a lot of reading and study because I was involved in teaching for the history of civilisation course which the whole school followed, and I learnt an immense amount about the ancient world. I am ashamed to say that, although I was now in my late twenties, this was the first time that I had really studied in detail the history and philosophy of Greece and Egypt, and I became extremely interested in Mycenae and Crete and in the kingdoms of ancient Egypt.

But I was also involved in teaching modern history; and for the lower sixth general I had to organise a course of civics and economics. For this too, I had to do a considerable amount of study. Anybody teaching history at Badminton really did have great scope. The headmistress, herself a mathematician, had tremendous faith in the power of the teaching of history and civics for making good citizens; she gave the subjects a generous amount of time on the time-table, and great encouragement to us who taught them.

After spending the first year of the war in Bristol, Badminton was evacuated to North Devon. We were fortunate that we did not have to move again as some schools did and we were free of air-raids. Even so it was an anxious time for staff and pupils who all had relations and friends involved in the war in one way or another.

One thing that I remember well about finding myself in a classroom, confronted with pupils, is how little I seemed able to achieve. I remember preparing lessons and finding that when the forty minutes had gone I had covered only one or two of the many points I had planned.

This is a beginner's hazard and is a reminder of how much people themselves develop and grow between their own school days and the comparatively few years later when they return as teachers. The very fact of having lived those few extra years, apart from the study that you have undertaken during them, does put you in a quite unexpectedly different position from the young people in the class.

When I began teaching I was staggered both at how little the girls knew and how slow they seemed in the actual physical task of writing things down. They were not stupid or backward girls—they must nearly all have been well above average in ability. In every new set of secondary school children coming on from their primary schools, teachers are surprised by this slowness which is one of the things that makes them aware of the vulnerability of their pupils.

A teacher has very quickly to learn what are the limits of a formal lesson time or study period. Frustration, disappointment and a falling off of interest follow if too much is forced on the pupil; on the other hand to accept that virtually nothing can be done and to give no opportunity for seeing some kind of advance, also produces disappointment and a falling off of interest.

Westcliff High School was a formal school and, as in most grammar schools, the day was divided into forty or forty-five minute periods; and in my subject, history, I rarely had more than two a week with each form, although as far as I remember I had six in the sixth; possibly I had three with the school certificate forms.

At Badminton we did some experimental work on having a longer period in the day for a concentrated section of the term. This was done for English, history and geography in the middle school—what we call the second to fourth years in the normal secondary school—and as a historian I had history with my second year group three mornings a week for three periods for a quarter of the term, while my English colleague was having the third year for the same block of time and my geography colleague the fourth year. We then changed round for each quarter, and for the fourth quarter of the term we had one week each. We all, I think, had one period or possibly two in addition to our block time with the other groups so that we could keep in touch with them.

To have, in a subject like history, three periods running three mornings a week with the same group is quite challenging but it does mean that real study can be undertaken and the girls can see quickly how much they have acquired and what interests

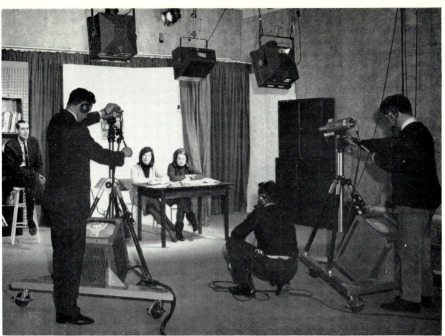

1 Postgraduate students gain experience with educational television, Leeds University

2 Map reading for a winter expedition

3 Marmalade, or an exercise in practical mathematics

4 A frieze for the form room

5
The weather observed
and recorded

6
A story dramatised

7 Teachers in training, St. Mark's and St. John's, Chelsea

8 Carol singing at the Royal Festival Hall

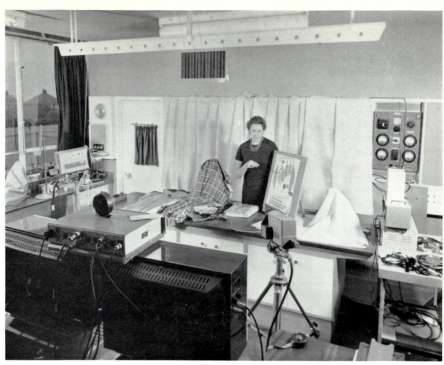

9 A lesson in dressmaking by closed circuit television

10 Student delegates at a model General Assembly of the U.N.

11   Pottery takes shape

CRAFTS AND SKILLS

12   Practical experience in an engineering shop

13 Teachers in train-
ing prepare visual
aids

14 A machine to help the backward reader

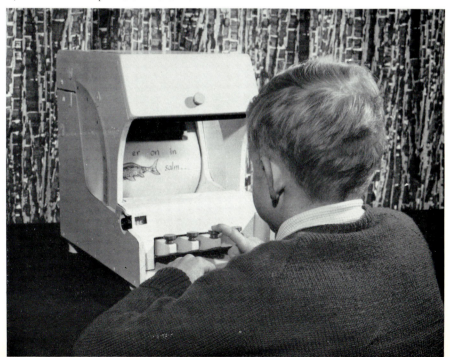

15 St. Crispin's, Wokingham

16 Mayfield

have been opened up to them. No doubt for some it was very boring but if it was boring for either the pupils or for the teacher, then we were not using the opportunity properly. I still think that there should be more opportunities in schools for this kind of organisation of time.

5

FACE TO FACE WITH COLLEAGUES

STAFF-ROOMS have changed enormously since I began teaching, particularly those in the older girls' secondary schools. When I started at Westcliff there were no men on the staff and as far as I remember the only married woman was a widow. There was a clause in my contract stating that I would have to resign my post if I married and this was typical of nearly all the contracts at the time. In any case there were far more women than men in the population so there were more than enough unmarried women.

As far as I remember, the conversation in my first staff-room revolved round individual girls, the agonies of marking, matters of school discipline, personalities of course—particularly that of the head of the school—and outside interests which consisted mostly of theatre, books and music. A normal opening for conversation at staff lunch would be 'What are you reading at the moment?' or 'What theatres have you been to?' or 'Have you been to the cinema lately?', for it was a period of very good films, and the cinema played a far greater part in most people's lives than it now does. Then we had no television although we did have sound broadcasting.

Nowadays the conversation in staff-rooms is rather different. I hear a lot about mortgages, about babies, about the cost of living, and this is natural since the majority of women teaching in girls' schools are now married. Not only are there married women in the staff-rooms but in many girls' schools there are men too, and my impression is that the staff-room is now a more natural place. It is not isolated from the world as the all-women staff-room tended to be.

I suppose there are always grumbles in staff-rooms. I certainly remember as an assistant mistress in the two very different schools in which I served, that one of the things that always bound the staff together was grumbling about the administration of the school, either the personality of the head or some regulations or arrangements which had been made! This does not necessarily mean antagonism and I was very fortunate not to serve under heads to whom there was antagonism, but it just seems to be assumed that the powers-that-be are there to be targets of criticism.

As a head I have always been conscious that this process must still go on and it is indeed one of the things that a Head has to prepare for and not to mind. She must be aware that she is under fire and criticism all the time, but must not allow herself to be emotionally disturbed by the knowledge.

But staff-room talk is not all grumbling and one really exciting and positive thing that does emerge is the extreme concern of nearly all teachers for the job that they are doing. It certainly is true that most sensible and progressive changes in the schools have come about, in the first place through casual and then perhaps through more formalised discussion.

One of the really enjoyable things about teaching is that you have colleagues who are like-minded and with whom you can share experience and exchange gossip at a level which really may be quite productive of ideas. The sharing of experience in varying teaching situations in a staff-room can be of immense value; the knowledge of how somebody else has coped with a certain group or a certain individual can help you to know how far you can go or what you ought to do.

Of course, there is a danger too that a pupil or a class can gain notoriety in the staff-room and sometimes a member of staff may feel that she must be different if she does not manage to have some story to add to the adventures of 3B or whatever the particular group may be; sometimes it is an individual who gets the treatment in this way, and this has to be guarded against.

But staff-rooms are not for gossip, they are really for working, and a great deal of paper work does have to be done by teachers in all kinds of schools. There is the inevitable and sometimes soul destroying marking of books. What is marking? Correcting, blue-pencilling, encouraging? Is it a good thing to do? Does it achieve anything? What do the children get from the marking? Unfortunately all too often what *they* want to know is your final assessment and they are much less interested in the comments in the margin and the suggestions for changes of spelling and arrangements that the conscientious teacher gives.

One of the good things that has developed in recent years is that most schools have moved away from competitive marking and placing in form, as though you were grading eggs and not children in the process of learning. But marking is something that makes great demands on teachers if it is well done.

I remember with great distaste the marking of examination papers. (They are so much more fun to write). This is partly because I very much dislike the whole technique of examinations. I had an enormous dose of marking when I first began teaching because my subject was history and we took the London General Schools Examination. We had a large number of girls who took the examination and they all had to write three hour papers. As we had two school examinations during the fifth year, one in December and one in March, I can remember now the hours and hours I sat up at night marking these scripts on Sixteenth and Seventeenth Century England.

The adding up of marks for papers like history seems to me one of the most uneducational things that history teachers have to do and I am always hoping that the hold of examinations will diminish as educational ideas develop. Unfortunately at the moment this is not happening and there seems to be more stress on examinations and examination techniques than ever before.

But the teacher in the staff-room and in her own time has not only got to mark examination scripts, she has got to study and prepare lessons. A lesson is something which has form, which needs thought. Even when the teacher appears to play little part, the lesson will be effective only if it has been well prepared and the teacher is able to guide the individual and groups towards the carefully prepared aims.

Two or three times a year large folders or envelopes containing Reports appear in staff-rooms, and writing the individual remarks on each girl's report takes a lot of time and thought. Some teachers make cogent and original remarks which really do help the pupil and the parents, but all too often the comments are stereotyped and rather dull.

Staff-rooms are usually untidy. There are piles of exercise books and text books, but it is extraordinary how a sort of detritus seems to accumulate in every staff-room in a school which is active and in which a lot of things take place. There are the models made by the mathematics classes which are left on the table, and these cuboid and spherical shapes mingle happily with the models of Shakespearian theatres, mediaeval manors and monasteries, and simple scientific circuits.

The science people are most successful at keeping their material away from the staff-room because the laboratory is well established as a teaching place, whereas the special mathematics and history rooms are still comparatively rare so that the teacher takes round her bits and pieces of apparatus with her. But far stranger things happen, because children do plays, and there are crowns and swords, stars and shepherds' crooks, and then there are pieces of stone and ore of various kinds which the geographers have collected.

Once a year, if the school has a fair or fête, other strange things will linger in the staff-room and mingle with the educational models; there will be felt toys and gingham aprons, decorations for the tea stall, and tins and boxes of all shapes and sizes in which money and contributions are collected. And then, of course, there is the inevitable lost property, pens, pencils, set squares, odd gloves and gym shoes, berets, scarves and rounders bats.

The fellowship of a good staff-room is something of immense human value; its quality affects the quality of the school. Because the members of the staff of any school share interests, it is natural that friendships should form and holidays be planned in addition to expeditions for the school. In mixed schools friendship often develops into engagement and commitment to marriage.

Possibly the most important thing that any member of a school staff gets is this sense of good fellowship. This is sometimes expressed in joint activities, for instance the staff plays which are always the most enormous success with all parts of the schools. Somehow the staff seem to be able to take off the dilemmas of everybody whatever position they hold in the school. There are staff teams, and I remember during the war when we were evacuated we had a staff play-reading circle, and it was through this that I came to know an enormous number of modern and classical plays.

But the staff are not only in a special relationship to one another, they are in relationship to teachers in all the other schools. It is a sad thing that teachers at the present day in England and Wales are not united in one professional union. This is because of the historical development of the teaching profession.

We have already seen how the two kinds of schools grew up quite separate from each other for many generations, the elementary schools staffed mainly by men and women who were two-year trained in training colleges, and the secondary schools staffed by university graduates some of whom were also professionally trained. Historically the teachers in the elementary schools were members of the National Union of Teachers, and the teachers in the secondary schools belonged to their own much smaller unions, the Association of Assistant Mistresses, the Association of Assistant Masters, the Association of Head Masters, the Association of Head Mistresses. This last group of four associations does try to speak with one voice, though not always effectively, through the Joint Committee of the Four Secondary Associations, known as the Joint Four.

There used to be a National Union of Women Teachers whose main object of existence was to get equal pay for equal work for women. This objective was achieved in 1961 when at last the pay of women teachers equated with that of men. The

National Association of School Masters opposed the women teachers' demand for equal pay but it did not dissolve when it had failed to stop them. It still exists as a powerful separate union.

This separation weakens the professional status of teaching and it is to be hoped that people going into the profession now will do their best to see the interests of teachers as a whole, and not just those of a particular section to which they themselves belong.

6

SOME THOUGHTS ON DISCIPLINE

ONE DAY RECENTLY a sixth former who had thought she wanted to teach came to tell me that she had changed her mind. She had met a young teacher recently starting work, who had confided in her that she had great difficulty in keeping order. 'There is no discipline' she had said, 'and so I cannot get on with my lessons'.

Not being able to keep order is a fear which puts off quite a lot of people who are considering taking up teaching. But should the problem of discipline loom so large? Can you really consider discipline in isolation? What in fact is discipline?

There are two uses of the word 'discipline', one academic, when it describes a branch of instruction or of academic or moral training, and the other physical, when it refers to military traditions. Interestingly enough, in the dictionary, I find 'discipline' described as 'a training condition, order maintained among persons under control or command as pupils, soldiers, etc.'

In school we should be concerned with academic disciplines, those disciplines imposed by the processes of learning, but actually schools are often obsessed by the military traditions of discipline. One often hears asked of a teacher 'Can she keep order?' Or of a school 'What's the discipline like?' And somehow this discipline is thought of in military terms.

The trouble about thinking of the army as a pattern for schools is that it at once assumes that children are a sort of permanent 'other ranks' rather than growing creatures of the same species and potential as their 'officers' and who may well outclass these same officers when they achieve adult status. You hear of people who have a 'gift for discipline', or that somebody ought not to be a teacher because 'she can't keep order'; but order and discipline cannot really be separated from what is actually being done in the classroom or in the school. If the teacher can help to create an atmosphere in which learning takes place, in which something is revealed, then discipline happens and order prevails.

One of the big educational changes which has taken place during the last thirty years is in the total approach to education, and this has involved less preoccupation with discipline. Education is now recognised to be concerned with activity and awareness: children play and through playing they learn skills; they become active, they ask and not only answer questions, and they are helped to understand processes rather than learn facts by heart. Discipline is a by-product of genuine activity.

What of the discipline round the school, though, apart from that in the classroom? In the old days, there were rules: 'Silence in the corridors', 'Walk in single file', 'No running'. These are all commands which many school teachers have been familiar with some time during their careers, and some people may still think that they, or similar rules, are necessary for the main-tenance of good discipline.

But what is discipline in school FOR? Surely it is simply to provide a framework of security, order and peace in which young human beings can grow and develop, and in which they can be protected. So that they can grow with the least possible pain there must be order, but it must be based on reason and on the needs of the individual and not on some external and irrelevant set of standards.

I can see no point in forbidding chidren to talk in the corridors or to walk in twos or to run, unless all these things interfere with other people. Running in school corridors can be dangerous and, indeed, walking in large groups can be dangerous, but the alternative is not a rigidly controlled, silent, single file, but a reasonable way of walking along in company without preventing people in the opposite direction walking along equally comfortably.

But discipline is more than an orderly way of walking about a building; the discipline or order of the school is reflected in the way its members speak and behave to each other, not only in the classroom but as they go about their business round the school. There is a civilised way in which human beings communicate whether the conversation is taking place between a teacher and a child, or one child and another one, or a young child and an older member of the pupil body, and a school must help its members to achieve this.

But there are problems of really anti-social behaviour: stealing, destruction of property, writing on walls, and things of this kind. How are people disciplined, if we must use the word, not to behave in this sort of way? Should the school teacher punish the delinquents and what form should the punishment take if she does? These questions are among the most difficult that teachers have to face.

The whole subject of punishment is a most complicated one. There can be no modern educationist who accepts corporal punishment as a suitable means of correction in schools, but what can you do or should you do?

Some research done a few years ago showed that of all the things which school teachers meted out as punishment to their pupils, the one that was most dreaded was not a talking-to by the head, or being kept in, or having to write lines, but having a letter sent home to the parents. But even so this has a different effect on different people, and I find that punishment has to be individual to be effective.

A 'talking-to' has a profound effect on some, but makes absolutely no impression on others. Being kept in can be an agonising restriction of liberty for one girl but is simply taken in her stride by another, and sometimes just becomes a habit. There was a fashion at one time for making defaulters write lines—'I must not be rude', 'I must not answer back', 'I must not run in the corridor'—and they had to write these lines hundreds and hundreds of times. Apart from the abuses that this led to, it has always struck me as being a very ineffective sort of punishment.

Then progressive people thought it might be better for the sinners to do something constructive, and suggested that perhaps some arithmetic or poetry should be studied, but, of course, the teachers of these subjects said that it was quite wrong that their subject should be turned into a punishment and that the best way to kill poetry and arithmetic was to give it as a punishment, and I must say that I share this view. Of course, if it is a question of punishment for bad work, then repetition of the work seems a logical and sensible task.

The trouble about making the punishment fit the offender rather than fit the crime is that other people seem to think that justice is not then done. 'Look', they say, 'she did it too, and she's not had a letter home'. So the administration of justice is difficult at school just as it is in the world, and I must say that in all the years I have been a head and an assistant teacher, I have been profoundly dissatisfied with punishment as a means of securing reform and consequently good discipline.

Somehow the individual has got to be helped to get back into the main swim, to realise that some misdeed has been done, and to make some sort of retribution for it, and punishment does not necessarily do this.

I should not really treat punishment and discipline together, because discipline is something positive and can be creative. It is an aid, whereas punishment is negative and preventive, something that we fall back on when discipline fails; and just as we saw that there were two kinds of discipline, so within the discipline that means order and training, there are still further sub-divisions.

There is discipline for the sake of the community; for example, people are asked not to walk along the corridor with linked arms, four or five abreast, because this prevents other people from walking along the corridor in an orderly and peaceful way. You can think of plenty of examples of rules and regulations which are made to discipline people in communities so that the lives of the majority of the community can be lived in comfort.

But then there is discipline for the sake of the individual, for example, discipline in the classroom, the aim of which is to maximise the efficiency of each individual for the task in hand. The earlier view was that the child was a passive recipient of the lesson, a process sometimes described as 'filling the pot'. The child was an empty vessel just waiting to be filled up with the knowledge and the wisdom of the teacher, and on this assumption it was considered reasonable that the children should be quiescent and that they should be 'disciplined' to be quiet and still so that they were ready to RECEIVE the lesson. Part of the outward show of this technique was the old elementary school tradition of making the children begin the lesson by sitting up straight, with hands on heads, or sitting on hands or something of that kind.

Psychological research has amply demonstrated that learning is most efficiently done through the active participation of the learner. The teacher's job is to see that the pupil learns rather than to pump something into the pupil. It has also been demonstrated that a living organism is essentially active and that efficiency is impaired if the child is restrained physically.

Adults themselves have learnt to control their physical movement so that they are in a state of apparent quietness when they are studying or listening, but a child who talks is not necessarily a naughty child; she may well be a child who can handle ideas. A child who fidgets and moves is again not necessarily a naughty child who needs to be disciplined, but one who can readily explore, investigate and create. These ideas have been put into practice by those teachers who adopt what are known as 'activity methods', and these have been particularly effective in primary schools in Great Britain during the last twenty or so years.

A school or a class which is organised on activity methods may seem to the orthodox observer to be untidy and noisy; there is a lot of movement, there is busy-ness, there is what appears to be restlessness, but this does not mean that there is not discipline. It may well be that in an ordered activity class there is more actual mental and personal discipline being exercised than in the quiet and 'good' class which was so much admired in the past.

The task of the teacher in this sort of situation is really more difficult than in the older one where her main aim was to keep order so that the children were subjected to her will and in this state of passivity received knowledge. The teacher, as the active stimulator of ideas, has got to be very much more aware of the different paces at which her pupils are learning, the different interests of individual children, the enormous number of ways in which people can interpret what has been said.

The fact that a class consists of thirty or so individuals means that there are thirty or so hearings and understandings of what the teacher has said, or what the book or the picture or the music tries to say. The teacher has got to be aware of the different levels and speeds of understanding of the pupils in her charge. Without this understanding there will be no discipline.

7

ON HISTORY, EXAMINATIONS AND TRAINING TEACHERS

I USED TO THINK history the most difficult of subjects to teach and to examine, but I enjoyed working on the theory of teaching it when I found myself responsible for 'history method' at the Department of Education in Bristol University.

As a teacher I had become more and more discontented with the traditional school history syllabus and more and more conscious of how very difficult history is to teach. For one reason there is so much of it; it goes further and further back because of more and more discoveries in archaeology and anthropology, and further and further forward as time marches on, and further and further outwards as distant parts of the world are brought nearer each other and the world becomes more interdependent.

I tried to devise a world history syllabus and began writing a textbook to go with it. I began by thinking one could start the eleven-year-olds with the present day and go back into the nineteenth century and then take a leap right back to ancient times. But one of the troubles of beginning with the present is that the present becomes the past so quickly that the book is out of date before it reaches the publisher's hands, let alone the teacher's hands and the pupil's minds.

I still do not know how to solve the problem of the history syllabus and I have recently been considering it again in the light of the needs of the pupils who are going to sit for the new Certificate of Secondary Education. Here is an opportunity to get away from 'O' level type history and to base the work on the pupils' interests and their school course.

When it comes to trying to examine the work one is up against a good many problems; indeed the whole question of examining is one which every teacher must think about very closely. In my first school where the work was fairly formal I had to spend quite a lot of time devising examination questions, as we had examinations every term, and this is a very difficult thing to do. There are so many different kinds of questions; the formal essay type, the single word answer, the multiple choice, the diagrammatic, and so on, all very interesting; but it is a great pity if the setting of examinations and preparation for examinations dominate the teaching in any school.

I have no objection to examinations as long as they are kept in their place and are used simply as a means of checking and testing and revising the work that has been done in a certain span of time. Once teaching becomes preparation for examinations, then education is lost sight of.

Of course, if you ARE undertaking teaching for examination purposes, you have got to do your best to get your pupils through their examinations. There is nothing more disheartening than a set of bad examination results, but I am still convinced that concentration on getting 'results' does not in the long run yield really good results. I know, for example, schools both primary and secondary, whose pupils do very well in their examinations but who seem to fade out at the next stage because they have not really been educated, but only crammed.

I spent two years in the Department of Education at the University of Bristol. This I found a most interesting and exciting thing to do and I particularly enjoyed the entry that my job gave me to so many different schools. Some of the students in the department for whom I was responsible were doing teaching practice in the new secondary modern schools, some were in independent and direct grant schools, and most in ordinary maintained grammar schools.

I was, to start with, very anxious and nervous as I wondered how on earth I could, in the first place lecture on history method when I had really found history very difficult to teach; and secondly assess the actual teaching of students who might be teaching any subject—geography or nature study or even mathematics.

In the event, however, neither of these tasks was as frightening as I had expected, and I gained a greater insight I think into the difficulties of teaching by going through with my students the agonies of getting the right proportions of exposition and question and discussion and private study, and the right approach and so on, than I had learnt from my own direct experience.

I found it particularly interesting to supervise lessons in subjects which I had not taught myself; the subject matter was usually of a simple enough nature for me not to have to worry too much as to whether I knew if it was actually correct or not. But the methods of teaching in a sense were easier to analyse in a subject that was not my own. I remember noting some of the dangers that the young teacher falls into and they reminded me of similar things I had done myself; for example, too much reliance on a particular textbook or authority.

I remember a geography lesson on life in Japan given to a group of twelve- and thirteen-year-olds in a secondary modern school. The lesson was based on a rather old-fashioned textbook which talked about the elegance and discipline and politeness of the Japanese and their great efficiency. The lesson was taking place at the time when the Pacific war was still at its peak and the Japanese were represented in our newspapers as being barely human.

I asked the student whether she thought that the pupils in the class would wonder at these two different pictures of life in Japan, and to my amazement she had not really worried about the difficulty herself. She had simply decided that this was something that she had to teach and had proceeded to teach it, really quite well, but with no awareness of or reference to the things that were happening all round her every day.

Another pitfall, and I suppose in a way it is another version of the same thing, was that of the student who clung to her syllabus for help but was also told to use the Schools Broadcast. When I arrived she had a double period and she was teaching about the Renaissance. This was going to be interesting, and particularly as she said that they had to break off in the middle for listening to the broadcast. I said, 'How interesting. Are they doing a series on the Renaissance?' She said 'No' about Wolfe and the taking of Quebec', so I said, 'Well, might it not be better to build the lesson round this?' She said, 'Oh, no! They have to keep to the syllabus.' 'Then', I said, 'do not have the broadcast.' She said, 'Oh, no, the Head says they must have the broadcast. And to my horror we solemnly sat through a rather formal listing of those events which define the Renaissance in school textbooks; the discovery of the compass, the voyages to the West, the printing press, the interest in ancient languages and so on, and then we solemnly broke off and listened to an extremely good dramatic version of Wolfe and the taking of Quebec. No reference was made to the background of this episode, and I cannot think what it could have meant to the unfortunate pupils.

As for my method lectures, I found that I was able, as a result of visiting lots of schools and seeing a good many students, to collect a very adequate supply of material to add to what I had gathered from my own teaching experience.

This opportunity to think about methods of teaching in general and to see many kinds of school in action formed a very useful preparation for being a headmistress.

8

ON BEING A HEADMISTRESS

IT WAS WHEN I was at Bristol that somebody suggested to me that I might apply for the headship of Pate's Grammar School for Girls. I had not really thought of myself as a head, but various considerations led to my putting in an application. For one thing, with other staff coming back from the war, I felt I would not really be needed in the Department of Education any longer, although Professor Fletcher told me that post-war expansion would ensure I was not redundant.

In addition to this my father had now had to give up work and I was concerned about finding my parents a home; so somewhat fearfully I put in for this post, and to my surprise I was appointed. It was fortunate that, as Bristol is fairly near Cheltenham, I was able to go to Cheltenham during the summer term and take some share in the time-tabling and appointment of staff for the following year.

It was not an easy time to take over as there had been an interim of two terms without a head when the school had been temporarily run by a retired H.M.I. and because of post-war changes generally there had been a great many changes of staff. Somehow the time-table got made and we started the Autumn term reasonably well; of course, as always in a good school, things go on in spite of the headmistress in the early stages of a new head's term of office.

At the beginning, therefore, I felt a little bit superfluous and it was only gradually that the magnitude of the job impinged on me. I can remember sitting on the platform and wondering how I should ever get to know all those 500 girls and staff. Little did I think then that I should one day be head of a school of 2,000.

I had followed the most obvious career line in teaching, that which leads to a headship, but there are other avenues of promotion. It is possible to become an inspector of schools, either for a local authority, or as one of Her Majesty's Inspectors, or a supervisor or organiser of a particular subject in an area, or one can go into educational administration or become a lecturer or principal of a College of Education.

It is odd that in England and Wales it is not necessary to take any special training to do any of these particular jobs. Many people who become lecturers in Colleges of Education have taken some postgraduate diploma or a higher degree, but for headships, the inspectorate and educational administration, most people go straight on from teaching with their original qualifications.

This is, I think, a weakness in the English educational system, but there are various opportunities for voluntary training and discussion about the responsibilities involved in taking on these jobs which are rather different from ordinary classroom teaching. The Department of Education and Science now organises courses for heads and the College of Preceptors, for example, holds courses on school administration addressed by heads and deputy heads, inspectors, and professors of education; these courses are extremely well attended by members of school staffs of all kinds, primary and secondary, who are looking for promotion within the school system.

In the United States there are much more clearly defined lines of promotion, and training courses are essential if you switch from one line to another.

Within the schools there is an increasing number of graded posts between that of being an assistant teacher and being a head. In the secondary field there are graded posts, which have a salary above the basic, given to teachers for special responsibilities held either in relation to the teaching of their subject or to some other school activity, such as careers advice and remedial work. Most big schools also have housemistress posts or posts with responsibility for a particular section of the school. This sort of experience is very useful for intending heads.

Then it is possible to become head of department and to be responsible for the organisation and teaching of a subject through-out the school, the preparation of the syllabus, the supervision of the work of the other teachers in the department, and so on. And there are senior assistant posts and deputy head posts, and the present salary scale allows for very large allowances for the most responsible of these posts. But the most obvious avenue of promotion is that from assistant to head of the school.

What happens between finishing one term as an assistant mistress and beginning the next term as the head of the school? From teaching one subject you find yourself answerable for all subjects. After coping with 2B2's problems in your own lessons, you are promoted to coping with the teacher who is failing to cope with 2B2's problems. After making claims for your own subject you have now got to answer the claims of all the other people. From criticising the placing of your own lessons in the weekly time-table you have to defend the arrangements made for everybody.

From being one of a team you suddenly find yourself the captain or the chairman or the president, the one who has to make the decisions, and instead of making criticisms or giving praise you suddenly find that you have to be ready to take both, and neither is easy.

My two years at Bristol made a most useful bridge for me between being an assistant and being a head. I had had to sit back and assess my own and other people's work, and I had met many heads of schools and H.M.I.s, and of course members of the staff of the Education Department, all of whom taught me a great deal. Even so, I was aware of a subtle change in my relationship with other teachers when I became a headmistress.

Mercifully school staffs are no longer sycophantic but they still often endow the head with far more power than in practice she has or ought to have. After nearly twenty years of being a head, I fully realise that a head is not a powerful person. She has the opportunity to influence the habits, attitudes, even the behaviour and the choices of the staff and the pupils, but this only if there is mutual confidence and respect.

In fact, just as the awareness of ignorance is frequently the beginning of wisdom, so the realisation of powerlessness is the beginning of the understanding of the demands of leadership. Even so, heads must recognise that they are in an unusual relationship to other people. I remember very well that slight and subtle change of temperature which can happen at the staff lunch table, or at a non-educational party when it leaks out that I am a headmistress.

This happens, of course, not simply because I am a head but also because of the difference between the teaching profession and all the other professions. Everybody has been to school, has been a customer as it were, and everybody carries a certain resentment against, or perhaps shyness, in the presence of those who saw them immature, silly, afraid, spotty, cheeky and so on.

A head does not have an easy rôle to play. I remember someone quoting once from Goldsmith about the village headmaster, *For in him we see oil, vinegar, sugar and saltness agree.* The quality that decides on the balance of oil, vinegar, sugar and saltness in the head is judgement, and this is something we do not acquire automatically on appointment as heads, and we never shall acquire it if the headship, the prestige, the power, that go with it are thought of as things worth having in themselves.

It is probably true that those who spurn power are best able to exercise it. In fact, being appointed as a head of a school is a humble-making experience and no one can be certain how she is going to make out. It certainly does not follow that a successful subject or class teacher will necessarily be a good head.

Indeed, looking back on my years as a headmistress I think it quite strange that we heads manage as well as we do considering that we have no special training in organisation, in management or in psychology; we just learn the job pragmatically and from the good, bad or indifferent practitioners under whom we have served; it is possible that as many good heads are made by rebellion and protest against a bad head as by copying a good one.

But you cannot just think of being a head in isolation, you have got to think of what you are a head of, and indeed the head is the centre of a whole complex of relationships. She is in special relationship to her teaching colleagues, to the administrative and domestic staff, to the pupils, their parents, the employing authority, the Department of Education and Science, and the neighbourhood and local community in which the school is situated.

She may be the king pin in all this in the purely engineering sense that it is her job to hold the parts together but she must not think of herself as the king pin in the popular slang sense. That way madness lies. There is no divine right of kings in headmanship. If the royal analogy appeals, it must be a post-1688 monarchy, a monarchy in which it is known to both ruler and ruled that power is vested in the king but by parliament.

I prefer to think of a school in republican terms, as a commonwealth of which the head is president or chairman, and a chairman who knows that there are other citizens who could fill her place as well and better than she can. A good chairman has to explain and make suggestions, listen to criticism and counter suggestion, and either lead the committee to come to a decision or, if it will not and cannot, come to a decision herself.

I am sure that a head's policy should be laid down only after consultation with her colleagues. That staff should be and should feel themselves to be included in policy making is a basic ingredient of good relationships. They will have to carry out the policy and they will do it better and more happily if they know they have had a share in its formation.

I became a head when I was still comparatively young, and I remember with gratitude and admiration the way my colleagues, many of whom were older and more experienced than I, rallied round and looked after me and helped me not to make too many terrible mistakes. Of course I was anxious and a bit afraid. Even so, I remember with a certain feeling of pleasure the sense of being on my own which goes with being in a position of authority.

If you are not prepared to accept this feeling of separateness and enjoy it, and use it in establishing your relations with the staff and pupils, I think it would be very difficult to take on the responsibility of a large school. There must be a sort of clinical detachment which separates a head from the school, as it does a doctor from his patients and indeed a class teacher from her pupils.

This does not mean that there will not be deep concern for and interest in individuals, but the concern must not become the kind of involvement which distorts judgement. It is important that a head does not allow her decision-making to be affected by a need to be liked; the point applies equally to the class teacher.

Taking prayers is one of my duties as a head which I enjoy least, although I have found it much more rewarding since we stopped assembling the whole school at the same time. I like meeting sections of the school and sharing with them impressions of some important event or anniversary, and although I do not think that talks from the platform make naughty girls good, there are occasions when the head can discuss with quite a large group moral principles which have been flouted by some section of the school.

I remember with pleasure many discussions with colleagues over such matters which have often led to very interesting comments on human behaviour, and there is always a pleasurable feeling of comradeship when there is a shared joke about an individual or an occasion. Sometimes you may have made a fool of yourself and if you can laugh WITH, this is all to the good.

More than once girls have written in essays or on the forms they fill in for the Careers Advisory Section of the Youth

Employment Service that they do not want to be just an ordinary teacher, they want to be a head teacher. One, I remember, went on to say that she would like to have a nice room like Miss Miles's with a radio and not have anyone to tell her what to do! I'm afraid she had not got a very good idea of what a head's life is really like.

It is still the tradition in English schools that the head is first and foremost a teacher rather than an administrator, and I think this is important. Since I became head of a very large secondary school I have been able to have rather more clerical and administrative assistance than I used to have as head of an ordinary sized grammar school and this has given me more freedom to concern myself with general educational problems and to keep a fair degree of direct contact with pupils.

I think that it is a good thing for all heads to have some classroom contact with some girls, although this is not always easy to arrange. There is no doubt that the classroom situation gives the head a knowledge of the girls which is subtly different from what she learns by the occasional individual contact or the mass, and to my mind not very effective, contact which takes place in the daily assembly.

But just as it is good for the head to be freed from matters of administrative routine, so she should also be freed from being concerned solely with matters of discipline. It is unfortunate if the pupils feel that they are sent to the head only when something is wrong and that the only utterances that come from the head are corrective. It is very important that the head should pass on the nice things about girls as well as the nasty ones, that she should be able to talk about positive and normal events and not only be concerned when something has gone wrong.

It is a sobering thought that the years a girl or boy spends in secondary school are as important as any period of their whole life, except the first five years, in forming attitudes. There is an enormous difference between the eleven-year-olds who are still little girls and the Upper Sixth who are poised, elegant and mature young women; in between come some of the third and fourth year girls who seem to be quite different from either of the other age groups.

During these formative years the background of the school, its values and its attitudes, the quality of its relationships, are possibly more important than what is learnt in the classroom, and though I do not think that the head is the school, yet a head certainly can do quite a lot towards emphasising what things are important.

Basic to all this is the appreciation of the importance of each individual girl, and in truly democratic thinking this means all the individuals not just the clever ones and the successful ones. It is very dangerous for the head or the staff to dismiss or reject girls who do not or can not conform to their ideas of what girls ought to be like. It is difficult not to sin in this respect, but a head and all teachers must recognise and appreciate the uniqueness of people, and help them to be the best that they can be in their own right and not in comparison with anybody else or with any artificially set standards.

The opposite pole to the isolation or detachment of the head is, of course, a lovely feeling of universality and of belonging to all the different branches of school life. In recent years I find that I have been blessedly weaned away from my own specialism and have had to take an interest in other things outside the classroom—in music, games, clubs, in dressmaking, in drama.

I like going to rehearsals of plays, reading magazine proofs, watching matches, and I find that the casual contacts made in these informal ways are of tremendous value.

I still have a great feeling of excitement and commitment when any group in the school has prepared some entertainment or exhibition or series of speeches or shared in some outside event, and I have seen some of the preparation and know what has gone on in the background. The sense of being part of it is very real and very rewarding.

I can put the school activities through which I have sat into two categories, those at which I have been in great anxiety lest we were not going to get through, and those in which I have sat in beautiful peaceful enjoyment with every confidence that the thing is good, that the people in it know what they are doing, and have been sufficiently imaginative to know how to project their ideas and so to get their audiences fully involved.

It might be thought that this sense of belonging to all parts of the school would be easier to achieve within the relative homogeneity of a grammar school than a comprehensive school. In fact, I find that the varied activities and courses in a large comprehensive school yield even greater rewards of this kind.

After nearly six enjoyable years at Pate's I decided I must move. I loved Cheltenham and the Cotswolds (I even acquired a golf handicap there), but I was quite certain that I did not want to stay in Cheltenham for the rest of my teaching life. I applied for and was appointed to Putney County Secondary School, Mayfield.

I did not know at the time, nor did my predecessor who was retiring, how soon the school was to be enlarged to become a comprehensive school and, had I known, I might not have accepted the post. It was fairly soon after my appointment that plans for the extension of five London grammar schools, including Mayfield, were announced, and I had to decide what to do.

After some initial hesitation and with considerable trepidation, I decided, with the support of the staff, that we wanted to take up this challenge and make the most of the opportunity of extending to all children of secondary school age the quality of education previously available only to the lucky twenty per cent who went to grammar schools.

I had for some time been unhappy about the way selection for secondary education worked, and had been interested in the discussions on multilateral schools which had taken place before the changes in secondary education brought about by the Act of 1944. For these reasons, I was able to overcome the fears and hesitations caused by the proposed size and complexity of the new school and my feelings of inadequacy to cope with the whole range of educational ability.

My first years at Mayfield, then, were not easy, because no sooner had I begun to get to know the existing school and staff than I was plunged into planning for the extended school. Work was begun on the new building which had been imaginatively designed at record speed by Messrs. Powell and Moya, in August 1953. We received our first comprehensive intake, four hundred and twenty eleven-year-olds, in September 1955. We also absorbed nearly three hundred twelve- and thirteen-year-olds who transferred to us from other secondary schools.

It is not surprising that, when I look back on 1954-5, I think of it as a long series of interviews of staff and pupils. We had to appoint about thirty members of staff, including a deputy head and several heads of departments. As so often when you have really accepted the necessity for a change, in the event it can be very exciting. Once the new school was launched, we all settled down remarkably quickly and found great satisfaction from the sense of purpose that permeated all our activities. After ten years, the satisfaction and the sense of purpose are no less.

9

OUTSIDE THE CLASSROOM

WHEN I LOOK BACK on my years of teaching I remember more
vividly things that happened outside the classroom than what
I actually taught. I have clear recollections of expeditions to
theatres, factories and the Houses of Parliament, of camps
and conferences and matches, of crises over sick or missing
children, and of taking air-raid shelter duty.

Teachers have always done this sort of thing but during the
1939-45 war when thousands of teachers were evacuated from
the big towns with their pupils, they experienced without
making any conscious choice, a great extension of their responsibilities. They had to travel long distances to unknown
destinations with their pupils, they comforted them when they
were ill or when they were homesick, they acted as billeting
officers, and almost as foster parents; in fact they became
responsible for the physical and mental health of their charges,
and the actual classroom teaching seemed to be a minor
occupation.

But at the same time that these extensions of the personal
responsibility of the teacher for the pupil took place, there was
also an extension of responsibility in actual teaching: more
activity methods mean more preparation of material and arrange-
ment of apparatus. These two tendencies have resulted, in the

years since the war, in teachers finding themselves involved in an enormous number of activities outside the classroom, some directly concerned with their teaching but others that seem, to some teachers, irrelevant.

To the routine medical inspection have been added BCG vaccination and polio vaccination and dental inspection.

There is dinner money to be collected and the serving of dinner to be supervised. There are national savings, there is work in the school library, and there is what can be described as welfare work when the teacher becomes involved in some moral, personal or family problem to do with the children in her charge.

To do all these things the teachers need help, and it is encouraging that some local authorities are providing schools with professional librarians, a proper staff of laboratory assistants, first-aid helpers, and much more generous clerical and secretarial help, than they have had in the past. Some schools are now employing counsellors, or advisers, as auxiliary staff. Teachers need these human aids, as much as they need mechanical aids, if they are really to fulfil their professional obligations in the modern context.

There are also services provided by the local authorities for the schools in general rather than for particular schools, and teachers can now call in the help of the educational psychologist, or the physical education organiser, or the child care officer, or in London, for example, the Care Committee workers. All these services enable the teacher to see the child as a total being, and not just as somebody to be taught in the classroom.

In boarding schools this care for the total child has long been very carefully considered. I remember when I taught in a boarding school that I felt very much concerned and often worried about being responsible for the girls when they were not actually being taught in the classroom. There they were, some of them for their holidays as well as it was war time, and whether we liked it or not we were concerned with their total development.

There is a big difference between the responsibilities of a teacher in a boarding school (most of which are independent) and those in a day school under the care of the local authority. On the whole, the girls who go to independent boarding schools come from homes which are materially well off and in many cases culturally rich as well. In most of our maintained schools, a lot of girls and boys still come from homes which are culturally not well endowed—mercifully there are fewer and fewer that are materially poorly off.

I felt when I taught at Badminton School that I played very little part in the education of some of my pupils because their intellectual gifts and their home background were really the source of their educational development, and as a teacher all I could do was to mind their growth, or simply to keep it going. I found that I wanted to go back into the state system where I thought I could give more to the children in my charge.

This is not to say that I did not enjoy my spell as a teacher in a boarding school. I have kept up with many of my pupils since, and enjoy their company. I also enjoy their rather caustic comments on some of the things that were done, as we thought for their good, in their schooldays.

It is possible to teach in a boarding school which is not an independent school, for some Local Education Authorities provide boarding schools, such as the Inner London Education Authority's Wolverstone Hall (for boys) in Suffolk, for children who especially need boarding education. One mixed comprehensive school in London runs a boarding house for such pupils.

One of the rewarding things about having been a teacher for a good many years is the contact with former pupils, and this becomes more interesting as you get older and your pupils have themselves caught up and overtaken you. Recently I have had some very happy reminders of my early days of teaching from former pupils, now teachers and lecturers whom I've come across in the course of meetings, discussions, conferences, up and down the country. There is a pleasant sort of bond forged by common experience in the same institution, and it seems to get stronger with the passage of time.

Nearly all teachers have some hobby or interest which they want to share with their pupils, and teaching is the job *par excellence* which enables you to carry on with hobbies and interests. There is a great personal satisfaction in passing on your skill, knowledge and enthusiasm to people to whom it is all new and who come to these things with an open mind and with the enthusiasm of youth.

When I was at school myself I spent most of my free time playing games. I was a keen hockey and lacrosse player in the winter and travelled many miles over East Anglia to play matches on Saturdays. In the summer I played tennis, and again the schools that we competed with for the East Anglian Cup were very far apart and we moved about a lot in order to get our matches.

I wish now, looking back on my schooldays, that I had had more other interests, and particularly that I had been encouraged to take up music. But at my school the only people who took music seriously were those who were particularly good at an instrument and who went on with special lessons throughout their schooldays. Music was not indulged in as a community activity nor as a source of aesthetic enjoyment.

When I became a teacher myself, I found that I did not want to spend my extra-curricular time on coaching games and I found other things more interesting. Drama was one and I did help with plays in my first job at Westcliff and particularly during the war when I was at Badminton and we were evacuated to the country. I think the first full length play we did was *Richard of Bordeaux*. The school was unsophisticated, we had no television, few films, no live theatre, and the girls were deeply moved by the drama and pathos of Gordon Daviot's play, even when the Earl of Devereux's helmet slipped at a most tragic moment.

Country and mountain walking, and learning about flowers and birds was another interest. As a child I had not been particularly fond of, or even very conscious of the country, perhaps because we lived by the sea and I loved the beach and the water. It was when I went to the Nansen Pioneer Camps during my first teaching job that I began consciously to enjoy the country, and later in evacuation in North Devon my taste for walking and for living out of doors was further developed.

Now I get great satisfaction from just being in the country or, when that is not possible, in the garden, and from trying to learn about how to grow and tend plants and trees. This sort of interest is one which a teacher has plenty of opportunity to pursue and to hand on to the younger generation through clubs, expeditions, youth hostelling and adventure courses. And incidentally there is nothing like a stint of weeding to help you get over a crisis day at school.

The report of the Central Advisory Council, *Half our Future*

(1963), the Newsom Report, suggested that pupils in their last year at school should attend in the evenings as well as the normal morning and afternoon sessions, so that they could acquire tastes for hobbies and interests which would help them to use their leisure well when they left school. These sessions might be conducted by teachers who could also be Youth Leaders; in any case they would demand from the teacher the extended sense of responsibility for her pupils which is exercised by the best boarding school teachers and by many day school teachers.

Many teachers already do many of the things suggested in the Newsom Report and organise activities and travel outside as well as in school hours. Expeditions from my own school during recent months include: two-week stays at I.L.E.A. rural centres, a day at a farm, a week-end's youth hostelling, ten days' skiing in Austria, day visits to Magistrates Courts, large stores and businesses, the British Museum and Natural History Museum, singing in Haydn's *Creation*, and playing in the London School Symphony Orchestra.

All this is in addition to home exchanges with France, Germany and Denmark; study journeys to Yorkshire, Dorset and Wales, and holidays in Switzerland. All these things are demanding and tiring for the teacher but those who undertake them find them rewarding because of their great value to the children, and also because of the new insights they gain into their pupils in a different setting.

10

TRAVEL AND TEACHING OVERSEAS

MOST TEACHERS like to travel; I suppose this is because they, more consciously than most people, want to go on learning and finding things out. And after all, school holidays do give more opportunity to travel than most people's holidays do.

Teachers' salaries on the other hand do not allow for luxurious travel, but there are ways of visiting other countries without enormous expenditure. The most obvious is by arranging an exchange with a teacher in another country. Teacher exchange with the U.S.A. and some Commonwealth countries is highly organised. Each exchange is expected to last for a year and a great deal of trouble is taken to match the exchangers and their schools.

It is more difficult to exchange with a European school, but it is sometimes done. Some schools give sabbatical leave to members of their staffs who have given long service and this gives a wonderful chance to have a whole term to pursue a special study abroad.

When I was an assistant teacher I spent much of my out of school time on camping and travel to do with the League of Nations Union Junior Branches before the war, and then during and after the war with the newly formed Council for Education in World Citizenship. I was not able to go to Geneva with the League of Nations Union groups before the war because I could not afford it, but I went as soon as I could manage it afterwards.

But earlier on I used to help with the Pioneer Camps in Devon. As a Guide at school I had enjoyed the camping that the Guides had taught me and this stood me in good stead at these less formal and very enjoyable Pioneer Camps on the edge of Dartmoor. I must say I much preferred washing in a stream on Dartmoor, where I took my own tent and acted as a leader or discussion group chairman, to coping with the hessian horrors of most of my Guide camps.

Then there were exchange visits. I once took a group of schoolgirls to Denmark. They were not girls from my own school but were a group that was organised by the headquarters of the League of Nations Union. In the event the leader was unable to go and I was asked whether I would take on the duty. I went, as far as I remember, without anxiety, although looking back on it now I realise that I did take on quite a big job. The girls stayed with families whose daughters had already been to England and I lived with a charming family who were very anxious to learn English. I did not have the Danish teacher to my home as I think she had already visited England, but I remember with great affection my host family who were so very kind to me.

During the war, travel was cut off completely. In Lynmouth, Badminton's wartime home, we had some very good conferences for teachers which the school generously organised on behalf of the newly formed Council for Education in World Citizenship. They were attended not only by British teachers but also by many foreign educationists who were temporary exiles from their own countries. There was also a Sixth Form Conference at Sherborne School, which I remember very well, when one of the great issues was the independence of India.

Although at the time the war seemed endless, looking back on it the five years went comparatively quickly, and when I first became a headmistress in 1946 travel to the Continent was just beginning again. I was lucky enough to go to Paris to discuss a UNESCO production on the teaching of history and then to take a C.E.W.C. group to Geneva, and when I came to Putney I remember I conducted a C.E.W.C. group to Rome. I had not been in Rome since I went for the N.U.S. in 1933 and I was delighted with the post-war Rome.

Nowadays there are all sorts of cheap and exciting ways of travelling and school parties fly the Atlantic, cruise to Greece or go by bus to the Soviet Union. It is practically much easier to travel and young people have much more money than we did.

Some teachers, of course, travel through the activities of their professional association. There is a world organisation of teaching professions to which are affiliated the international federations of primary and secondary school teachers; and, as in all other international organisations, the scope of these unions is being widened enormously. Between the wars they were very much Europe centred and dominated, as was the League of Nations, but in recent years they, too, have become world wide and they hold conferences in Africa, Asia and the Americas, as well as in Europe.

There have always been many people from the British Isles who have wanted to go and teach overseas, and in the past missionary societies, and organisations such as the Society for the Overseas Settlement of British Women, have sent teachers to the countries that used to be part of the Empire and then the Commonwealth, and also to some countries outside, such as China.

Nobody forecast the tremendously rapid development of the

former colonial countries during the last ten years, but the leaders of these countries are very well aware of the enormous importance of education in this process of growth. Their people are hungry for education, and everybody who has taught in Africa tells of the extreme earnestness of the students and the self sacrifice, courage and sheer hardiness that has to be exercised by them, since they often travel many miles across difficult country in order to attend school.

Most local authorities nowadays encourage teachers to take jobs overseas and they make very favourable arrangements for secondment and return to a comparable job when their commitment abroad finishes. These arrangements stem in many cases from the findings of the Commonwealth Educational Conferences.

The first Commonwealth Educational Conference met in Oxford in 1960 and as a result of this great gathering of educationists from all the Commonwealth countries, Commonwealth Fellowships were created by which postgraduate students from developing countries could get higher degrees in the developed countries; teacher training bursaries were also provided by which a certain number of teachers from less developed countries go to the more developed countries to take advantage of the opportunities for training that these provide. The plan is that they then return to their own countries where they in turn train teachers from among their own people.

I was fortunate enough to be a delegate to the second Commonwealth Educational Conference which met in New Delhi in 1962. I sat on Committee B which dealt with the training and the supply of teachers. We in the United Kingdom delegation were concerned with the provision of the most suitable teachers for the jobs available.

It is interesting that we found some difficulty in persuading our colleagues in developing countries that a teacher from a three-year training college course in the United Kingdom, who probably had already got some 'A' levels before she went to college, was a very suitably qualified person to teach in junior secondary schools. Unfortunately, the mystique of the graduate is very strong in Africa and India; this is partly a legacy of British rule in the past.

There is no doubt that a good trained teacher is a very much more valuable asset in a developing secondary school than an untrained graduate. Personalities count, of course, and an individual graduate might be better than an individual college trained teacher, but by and large the college trained teacher has more to offer. It happens, of course, that people of similar status from the United States are graduates, and it is sad if United States graduates are preferred to English college trained teachers simply because they have the label of a degree.

In fact, one of the difficulties of co-operation in educational matters which emerges in all International Educational Conferences is this question of the equivalence of degrees. Colleges which I visited in Delhi, where girls were taking the first part of their first degree, were very similar to what we would call Sixth Forms or Sixth Form Colleges, and the work that they were doing for their inter- or their final B.A. or B.Sc. degree compared pretty closely with advanced level work in English secondary schools.

In 1964 the third Commonwealth Educational Conference met in Ottawa and the schemes for educational co-operation were developed still further.

It is certainly true that for several years ahead there will be great opportunities for young teachers to go abroad and give their services in different parts of the world. It is important to have some teaching experience in the United Kingdom first; a two-year spell of experience after completing a professional training or a concurrent training in a College of Education is undoubtedly good preparation for any kind of venture overseas.

Of course, since the development of Voluntary Service Overseas and International Voluntary Service many young people have a taste of teaching abroad before they actually go up to college. At Mayfield we were very excited and proud when one of our head girls was selected for V.S.O. in its early years. She went to Malaya and taught both in a girls' boarding school and in a village school.

This is another way in and, for some people, undoubtedly a highly successful one; young men and women discover talents and skills in themselves of which they were unaware, and having been put to the test in unusual and challenging situations they can come home and take their training or degree course with a much greater awareness of other people's attitudes and of what the whole thing is about than if they go straight from school.

I am fairly certain that if I were in the first ten years of my teaching career I would want to go abroad and to try my hand at teaching in and learning about some other part of the world than that in which I was brought up. For my generation the time that we might have been doing these exciting things was, of course, the period of the 1939-45 War. If you had taught for a certain number of years before the war, I think it was four or five, I cannot quite remember, you were in a reserved occupation and you had to stay at your job.

It is ironical that for some of us our late twenties were spent deep in the countryside of our own England or Wales, evacuated with our charges away from the great centres which were liable to be bombed. I was fortunate in that I was serving then in a school which had a strongly international outlook, and during these years of evacuation down in North Devon we tried as far as possible to keep in touch with people from overseas, but there was no question of serving abroad then, unless, of course, you were in the armed forces or other overseas services.

It was wonderful to be able to travel again when the war was over and I particularly enjoyed returning to France. But by this time I had acquired heavy home and professional responsibilities which made it difficult for me to think of getting a job overseas.

II

FACE TO FACE WITH PARENTS

Now THAT I have been a head for some time 'my' parents seem
to get younger and younger. When I first became a headmistress,
most of the parents of the girls in the school were older than I
was, and I suppose I identified them with parents of people that
I knew. When I came to London, 'my' parents were about my
own age and I thought of them as contemporaries. Now most
of 'my' parents are a good deal younger than I am and now I
identify them more with their children.

In fact it is frightening to realise that in spite of the comparative
inexperience of young heads, parents do tend to look to them as
father or mother figures, a collective parent, as it were, and
as schools become more and more concerned with the total
development of children and not just with teaching them a body
of knowledge, this aspect of the headmistress's life is enhanced.
Interestingly enough it is enshrined in law by the judgement which
said that a school should exercise in break and dinner hour
and so on that amount of control that a reasonable parent might
be expected to exercise.

There are, of course, official contacts with parents through a
Parent-Teacher Association or a Parents' Association. I think I
prefer a Parent-Teacher Association which by its very name
emphasises the fact that teachers and parents have joined together

to promote the welfare of the children in the school setting. Also in a Parent-Teacher Association there is a committee of both parents and teachers who can learn a lot from each other, whereas a Parents' Association can sometimes become an association of parents 'on the other side' from school as represented by the teachers.

In the past many heads have been very much opposed to Parents' Associations because they were afraid that the parents might interfere with the running of the school and make things very difficult for the head and staff. This seems to me an unreal fear because whatever the name of the association is, its success as an instrument in promoting the welfare of the children in the school depends on the sort of relationships which are established between parents and teachers.

In my experience the activities of a Parent-Teacher Association fall roughly in three parts. There are: first, joint enterprises, sometimes for the benefit of the school in the way of fairs and jollifications of one kind or another, perhaps to raise funds; and secondly, joint meetings at which educational problems are discussed, lecturers invited, films shown, and so on.

And then there is a third function which is the actual discussion by teacher and parent of the progress and attitudes of individual girls. In my experience the last activity is by far the most popular among parents. Some schools have Parents' Associations which organise social functions quite apart from the school simply in order to raise money to give things to the school. This seems to me a pleasant enough activity but does not replace the essential educational functions of a Parent-Teacher Association.

Then, there are meetings of parents which the head and the staff call when they want to impart some information or give some guidance to the parents about the next stage in their children's education. I find that these rather larger meetings, at which it is hoped to get as near 100% attendance as possible, take place at roughly three stages in the pupil's life.

At Mayfield we see all the parents when the children have first been admitted to the school. We see them again when they are about thirteen and have got to make choices about their future courses and subjects; and then at round about sixteen when it is a question of the sixth form with all its variety of activity and choice, or of employment or further education or training.

These meetings make great demands on the teachers, but in my experience they feel that the contacts they make and the insights they gain by talking to parents are of immense value.

Very important are the individual meetings between the teacher and the parents. All too often these are sought either by the parent or by the school because something has gone wrong. Parents ask if they can come and get advice from the school about how to cope with Mary, who is showing signs of rebelliousness, defiance and all sorts of anti-social tendencies at home. Sometimes the boot is on the other leg and the head asks the parent to come to school because the school is dissatisfied and unhappy about Mary's attitude. Sometimes she has been discovered truanting or stealing, or simply never doing any work, or always being late.

It does seem a pity that so many individual interviews with parents are a result of anxiety on one side or the other. They have nevertheless immense value and it is important that the ordinary assistant teacher, in the guise of tutor or form mistress or house mistress or year mistress, should also meet the parents of the children who are causing her anxiety. Parents are often amazed at meeting Miss or Mrs. So-and-So after they have heard the descriptions of her given by their off-spring.

It is in these individual interviews with parents that the head and indeed the assistant staff do so often have to be social workers as much as teachers. If there have been behaviour problems in school and the parent comes, it is invariably revealed that there has been some difficulty and disturbance at home, and those are sad days indeed when one after another of these tragic breakdowns in personal relationships is revealed.

The child of course is not an isolated individual who has suddenly decided to be naughty, but a person who simply has lost her basis of living and her security. She does not know whose side she is on and wonders why her home should be wrecked. I have frequently been astonished at the burdens of other people's mishandling of their affairs that have to be carried by so many school children. Sometimes school is the only secure place for these children, and here again it is vitally important that the teacher should see education as a total thing and not just as instruction.

Then, of course, there are paper contacts with parents. An occasional bulletin written in a friendly way to the parent about things that are going on in school, about changes in uniform and the reasons for them, new rules and dates of holidays and examinations; all this sort of thing needs to be communicated to the parent and the more personally it can be done the better.

An important change that has taken place in the schools recently is that whereas men teachers have almost always also been parents, now most of the women teachers are parents or potential parents as well, and I think that this makes a subtle

difference in the relationship of the teachers and the parents
when they meet.

One last kind of personal interview between the parent and
the teacher comes when the parent comes up to school to complain.
Sometimes the complaint is because Mary is always being 'picked
on' by a certain teacher and the parent demands that this dis-
crimination should stop. Parents are often surprised by the answer
that it is unlikely that she would be 'picked on' continuously unless
she is doing something to attract the attention of which being
'picked on' is evidence.

Sometimes parents complain about what they consider an
unfair punishment, and sometimes the child (and this I always
find it difficult to understand) has really misled her parents about
what has happened and yet not tried to prevent her mother
from coming to school. You would think that she would know
that it would all be bound to come out if the mother did come.

Sometimes the parents automatically take their children's side
and think that the teacher must necessarily be wrong. This is
rather a difficult situation to cope with and, oddly enough, in
my experience, I find that many parents who do come in the
early stages of a girl's career to complain that she is always being
punished or picked on, also come later on to say that something
has happened at home and to ask that we punish Mary for her.

This inability to have a detached judgement about their own
children is not general, I think, among parents, but is a very
frightening thing when it is carried to excess. I have had within
a very short time several instances of a parent coming up to
complain of our criticism of her daughter, about which she has
only known through the daughter's eye view, and then coming
soon after to tell me about something that the child has done

at home and ask for our help.

The most depressing interviews with parents are those when the parent refuses to admit that the child is in the wrong and the child leans on this very spurious parental support. In that case I have often found myself standing as firmly as I could on the position as it had been reported to me. Then I am threatened that one of three things will happen to me: the parents will go to 'the Education', or they will take it further, or they will 'get the law on me'.

I find these threats distasteful and they make me unhappy, but I have never actually been seriously affected by them. I often remember how my first headmistress told me when I was an assistant that if and when I became a head I would have to develop a very thick skin, 'the hide of an elephant' she said. I do not think that I agree with this advice, because I think that if your skin is so thick that you are unaffected by the darts which come from the difficult and unco-operative parent, or indeed when you find yourself in a position which perhaps is difficult to hold, it is no good just brazening it out. You have to have an element of self-criticism and wonder how the situation could have been avoided, and this, of course, is exhausting. It is the kind of thing which makes teaching in its most responsible form so very demanding. I think it a danger if the teacher's skin is too thick; but, though sensitive, it certainly has to be strong.

So being face to face with parents is certainly part of the teacher's job—nice parents, nasty parents, kind parents, cruel parents, considerate parents, inconsiderate parents. Parents are people and they provide the background from which the children come, and undoubtedly getting to know and understand the parents of the girls in the school is a very important part and a very interesting part of a teacher's work. Sometimes though you do feel after the end of the day that really the last people who ought to have children are parents!

12

ON GOING COMPREHENSIVE

THE MOST EXCITING and rewarding part of my career as a teacher has been the ten years since I have been head of a comprehensive school.

In future many secondary schools will be comprehensive, and so if you are still at school and are thinking of teaching in a secondary school, sooner or later you will probably find yourself teaching in a comprehensive school.

At my interview for the headship of Putney County Secondary (Grammar) School, as Mayfield then was, I was asked what I thought of the idea of a large comprehensive or multilateral school. I think I said that my previous experience had made me very critical of the selection processes and that on the whole I was the sort of person who welcomed change, but that I was frightened of the proposed size of the school.

Experience since then has exorcised the demon of size for me and I have come to realise that you cannot isolate size as a thing that is good or bad in itself. In 1954-55 Mayfield was a school of about five hundred and fifty girls; in the summer of 1955 a hundred girls left from the top of the school and they were replaced in September at the bottom of the school by over four hundred eleven-year-olds.

We also welcomed some two to three hundred twelve- and

thirteen-year-olds who were transferred from other secondary schools, and we opened in September 1955 with about one thousand two hundred and fifty girls. The following year we reached one thousand five hundred, then one thousand eight hundred, and in 1958 we reached two thousand. Each total in turn was accepted and found to be manageable.

Most of the difficulties we experienced as we grew resulted not from the total size but from the awkward shape of the school. At first the junior part was much bigger than the senior; for example, when we were about one thousand five hundred, more than half the school were only eleven or twelve years old, but by 1962, when the first admissions of 1955 had been right through their seven years, the shape of the school had become more orthodox and as the larger numbers reached the top we were able to reduce the numbers admitted at eleven. We now take about three hundred and sixty eleven-year-olds each September, whereas at one time we took as many as four hundred and fifty.

Our experience has shown that what is important in a school is not the total size (a fact of which most children in most schools are unaware) but the actual size of the immediate teaching and social group. It is odd how much passion has coloured the discussion of the size of the comprehensive schools when what people really ought to get passionate about is what goes on inside them.

This in turn depends on who goes to them, and here we get to the heart of the matter. A comprehensive school is one to which all the children of secondary school age in the neighbourhood come without tests or examinations; it is, as it were, an open-ended school, one in which no assumption is made at the age of eleven as to the length or type of any child's education.

Each September, when our new three hundred and sixty

members join us, they are divided into forms of about thirty, not rigidly streamed according to ability but in two broad bands; half the second band—and the forms in this group include the children who on the whole think more slowly—have form teachers instead of specialists for a good many of their subjects, but in *all* the forms the girls learn a foreign language, and they all take mathematics, not simply arithmetic, and general science, in addition to their ordinary school subjects.

In the second year some may add a second modern or classical language, and in the fourth year they each embark on a programme which they have chosen, which may include practical, academic, examination and non-examination subjects. The choice is made in consultation with parents and teachers in the light of the achievement and interest which the first three years have revealed; 'getting a grammar grading', 'passing the eleven plus', or any other of these odd results of selection are quite irrelevant when it comes to making these choices at the age of thirteen or fourteen.

At Mayfield we have become so used, as have many other comprehensive schools, to 'eleven-plus failures' going on to Ordinary and Advanced level and to university and colleges of education that we cease to exclaim about it.

But it is not only in the academic field that the 'eleven plus failure' plays a considerable part in the school. In the early stages of the comprehensive school people often used to ask me, 'But don't you find that it is the "grammar" girls who run everything and do everything?' Experience certainly has shown this not to be the case. Many people who have played distinguished parts in school, year and form plays, who have led the orchestra, played in teams, been senior prefects of outstanding quality, have been girls who did not get a grammar school grading at the age of eleven.

Given the opportunity to stay on at school beyond the leaving age of fifteen, the vast majority of boys and girls want to do so; they want to contribute to the community and they want to go on learning and are very glad to use the opportunities that the longer school life gives.

The staff of a comprehensive school is an interesting and exciting group to belong to. First because its size ensures that there will be other people with your interests and qualifications and you will not be on your own having to defend your subject or discipline against other more established or more powerful interests. Secondly, and perhaps paradoxically, it is interesting because its size also ensures that there are a lot of people with different interests and qualifications from your own, so that the staff society is one of great variety.

I have found that people who teach in comprehensive schools feel they are doing a tremendously worth while job, and they certainly have to carry great individual responsibility. Form and group tutors must know the children in their forms, they must decide when the head or housemistress or welfare people should be consulted, or parents written to. They must guide their charges in their choice of course and see that they are able to cope when they have chosen. And then because the school is not geared entirely to examination work, there is room for considerable individual initiative in trying out new syllabuses and teaching techniques, in organising school journeys, expeditions, camps, and so on.

It is, I suppose, certain that if we have a number of large schools in place of a greater number of smaller schools, there will be fewer headships, although the increase in population is, in fact, going to need a bigger total number of schools anyway, of whatever size. But even though there may be fewer headships, there are tremendous opportunities for promotion and for holding really responsible posts at a fairly young age inside the comprehensive schools.

In Mayfield our deputy head acts as an alternative head, rather than as an assistant, and has full responsibility for quite a large part of the school and of the school organisation. The senior mistress, the year mistresses, the heads of departments, all have jobs which demand an amount of judgement and dedication which is probably equal to what is required in some headships of smaller schools. The staff of most comprehensive schools are also helped by better office equipment and secretarial staff than secondary schools have been used to having in the past; and this again does increase efficiency and give dignity to the actual organisation of the school.

Many people who have not been into comprehensive schools continue to think that a large school must be an impersonal place, but this is not necessarily so at all. I find a real feeling of friendliness and excellent personal relationships in the large schools that I know, most of all in Mayfield which I know best. The girls do feel that they belong to their school and they are proud of it; they talk about it to doctors, hairdressers, people in shops and so on. Some of the things they say come back to me and they are nearly always things which I am glad to hear. Girls come and see us after they have left, and children in the junior schools, who get their ideas from their predecessors who have already come to the large school, seem very keen to follow them here.

Mayfield is a girls' school, but many comprehensive schools are mixed and in such schools there is even more opportunity for initiative and enterprise. Drama, music, school journeys, all profit from being part of a mixed community, and engineering workshops, which are not usually found in girls' schools, add to the facilities which are available to girls as well as boys in the mixed schools.

It seems to me that the comprehensive school is the logical step forward in secondary education in the second half of the twentieth century, for it is doing for all the boys and girls of secondary school age the same sort of thing that the secondary (now grammar) schools did for the twenty per cent who were lucky enough to go to them in the first half of the twentieth century; that is, giving them a good education suited to the needs of the society in which they are going to live.

This does not mean that comprehensive schools must give to everybody the literary and academic kind of education that the grammar schools gave to a minority; but that they should give to everybody opportunities equal to, though not identical with, those which were formerly given to a few. This means an enormously wide choice of subject and course to suit all the different sorts of people who now come into the schools. The older subjects still go on but they are often interpreted very differently, and alongside them the practical, artistic and aesthetic subjects are ranged with equal appeal and status.

One thing that follows from this is that rigid subject teaching tends to break down and this movement is another of the factors which I think appeals to young teachers. There is no doubt that teaching in a comprehensive school makes you challenge your own assumptions about what is suitable as the content of the secondary curriculum and what is practicable in method. Indeed, one of the healthy things about such schools is that it underlines the tremendous importance of teaching *people* rather than *subjects*; still more, helping people to learn rather than teaching them a body of knowledge.

I have just read a definition in an article on comprehensive schools which perhaps sums this up: 'To encourage a child to develop as he may instead of imposing on his development a predetermined shape and limit, is the basic idea of the comprehensive school'.

From this idea several developments follow. In the first place, the comprehensive school helps us to get away from the idea that academic ability is the only good. Tremendous personal development follows when girls and boys are able to follow a vocational bent against a background of general education. For example, at Mayfield we have a course in trade catering, and the girls who undertake this course at the age of fourteen really do study the craft of the catering trade and have to work under the same conditions as they would in a restaurant or hospital kitchen. It is extraordinary how personality and general learning and confidence develop along with the acquiring of a skill.

You see this too in commercial work; understanding accounts, acquiring skill with office machines, learning something which is going to give confidence and status to a girl when she eventually leaves school, all help personal development. These practical courses help to bridge the gap between school life and the much harsher world of trade and industry.

If you teach in a comprehensive school then, you will not be teaching in a sort of factory which is an agent for changing society, but you will be teaching in a school which has come into being to meet the needs of twentieth century society; a society which has changed and is changing very rapidly and for which the narrower selective education, formerly associated with the word secondary, is no longer suitable.

It seems to me absurd, therefore, to see the expansion of a secondary grammar school into a comprehensive school as the destruction of the school. It is not murder, but cultivation, to bring a school up to date and to remodel it to meet modern needs.

I often take visitors round Mayfield and although I usually enjoy these excursions I sometimes have a slight feeling of apprehension. This probably dates from an occasion when a very senior member of Her Majesty's Inspectorate brought to see us some distinguished educationists who were attending a Council of Europe Conference in Oxford.

We set out as usual, but I chose the route badly and we soon got the impression that there were hardly any girls in the school at all! It was the day IR were spending on a farm and some other first forms were at ROSPA House; the fourths were distributed between Billingsgate, a dairy and a hospital and a large number of seniors had gone to a C.E.W.C. conference.

Later, when we entertained some Dutch teachers and inspectors, I was luckier. As we went round the school, I noticed once again what lively and independent teachers we have. It is due to them that I experienced the usual glow of pleasure and excitement I feel when I see the girls involved with enjoyment and concentration in so many different activities.

We heard some second formers speaking quite fluent Russian, we saw some upper sixth formers concocting glazes for their Advanced level pottery, and some new first years learning how to use the Library. Some lower sixth girls were having a discussion on scientific method following a television programme, the catering girls were preparing a lovely lunch and had just made the bread rolls for it, some second formers were studying the theory of sets and some fourths reading Latin for pleasure.

The glass panels at the side of the classroom doors showed our visitors that there were lots of other things to see and hear if time permitted, but it did not and we had to ignore the sounds from the music rooms and the smells, both nice and nasty, from housecraft rooms and laboratories.

So you see that there will not be a dull moment when you teach in a comprehensive school.

13

WHAT NEXT?

IT IS CERTAIN THAT all of you who are now thinking of teaching as a career are going to be very much needed in the years ahead. You will be joining an expanding and important service, a service which is commanding more public interest than ever before.

This growth of interest in education is due partly to the now generally high standard of living, to full employment and to the existence of a society which has overcome the basic problems of poverty and ignorance for most of its members: a society which looks ahead to providing an increasingly sophisticated, and incidentally increasingly costly, education for everybody; the sort of education enjoyed by only a proportion of the public in the past.

Another of the reasons for this interest is the expansion in the sheer size of the education service made necessary by the population increase. There were 7 million children of school age in 1963 and there will be $9\frac{1}{2}$ millions in 1976, and $10\frac{1}{4}$ millions in 1986: this means that the school population will have doubled between about 1955 and 1986. This is due partly to a rising birth rate, but also to the increased length of school life, which many are already enjoying voluntarily, and which will become compulsory for all in 1970/1.

The fact that there are so many more people wanting education and that there is a greater public interest in it than ever before means, too, that it costs far more. Not only are we spending a greater amount on education but also a higher proportion of public money is allocated to it. A large part of this money is invested in improved school buildings and in the better material provision which is now demanded through the whole of the school system, but much goes towards the payment of teachers. The growth in the school population obviously demands an enormous expansion in the numbers of teachers.

In training colleges the number of entrants has risen from just over 5,000 in 1944, when the Clearing House was established, to about 30,000 in 1965, and will rise to a planned 40,000 in 1971: within the last few years the numbers entering training colleges have gone up by some 2,000 every year.

The university population has expanded steadily at the same time. Because of this, applying for admission to the university or to a College of Education is now a much more complicated and hazardous process than it was in my day; but the Central Register and Clearing House for the Colleges of Education, and the Universities Central Council for Admissions help both you and the institutions to which you are applying.

Many universities and all training colleges send for the candidates for interview. It is becoming less customary, however, for universities to interview everybody, probably because of the enormous burden placed on their staffs by the necessity to interview many hundreds of candidates when, in fact, the admission will be decided not so much by interview, or even by school reports, but by examination results.

We still in this country have a great respect for the interview as a means of selection. My own view is that this is rather dangerous, and that an interview even between a candidate and several members of a board or selection committee need not necessarily tell the selection board what they want to know, and in any case it is not always very clear what they *do* want to know. I have every sympathy with those universities who have dropped the interview as a means of selection but who do invite the students to see the university.

After three or four years at the college or university to which you applied so anxiously, you have to consider applying for a job. Schools and local authorities use various methods of selecting staff. It is possible, and this happens to the majority of students, to be interviewed by and to be appointed to one of the education authorities. Alternatively, it is possible for students to apply in response to advertisements directly to schools.

As a head I have been able to exercise two different ways of appointing staff—in my first headship I appointed my own staff and then reported to the governing body and the authority, and in my second school the staff are appointed by the governors. I do not feel it a restriction on my freedom to have the governors' help in appointing staff. I would often find it very difficult to make up my mind about a candidate on interview only.

When I was first a headmistress after the war there were so few candidates that I hardly ever had to make a decision and was lucky to find somebody to fill the post; that has sometimes been the case since, but on the whole in recent years for certain posts there have been quite a lot of candidates and in these cases I have always found it helpful to see the candidates with other people.

But I do not think that the formal interview with a group of people is the best way of discovering whether somebody is suitable or likely to fit in to the job in question, and I always like to have longer with the candidate first and to give her the chance to meet some of the other staff, and to see the school. From the point of view of the candidate I imagine that things are much eased by being able to see the school first.

For my own first appointment I had a rather unusual interview as I came back from my job in Switzerland especially for it. My train was delayed by an avalanche and I got to Westcliff only just in time. Incidentally I was paid for my travel expenses only within the British Isles, that is from Dover! There was a large committee to make the appointment. I do not remember whether I enjoyed it or not: I expect not, as I did not enjoy the interviews I do remember—and I certainly do not enjoy interviewing other people.

But the interview happens after you have made an application and it is important, when you see the sort of post you want advertised, that you set about sending in your application in an informative and well organised way. The importance of writing letters, filling up forms correctly, acknowledging invitations to interview, and offers of posts, seems fairly obvious, but it is remarkable how many people, even some already in the teaching profession, appear vague about some of these matters.

It is important not to give the head of the school the impression that you are doing her a favour by coming, although with the present shortage in certain fields this may well be so! You must try at an interview to answer the questions not in monosyllables, but also not in such a way as to give the impression that you are the interviewer. It is also important to make up your mind as to whether this is the sort of job you want and to find out about it before putting in an application. I think you owe it to the school to which you are applying to get yourself informed about what sort of a school it is.

Of course, all too often it is not so much an individual school as an area that people want to go and teach in. If this is so, it is as well to be quite open about it and to say that you hope that you will get the job, partly because this is where you want to live, or this is where your fiancé lives, or whatever it may be.

As an interviewer I have been disconcerted when candidates have made their personal lives the *sole* reason for wanting to apply for a certain job. I think that there has got to be some professional thought behind any application, and if the situation in the school also fits the domestic needs of the candidate so much the better.

But getting your job is not the end. It is another beginning for you but now you are no longer at the receiving end. Even so, teaching is a job in which you have to go on learning; at least you get most satisfaction out of it if you do go on learning.

If you are keen on your own academic study, be it history or science or mathematics, teaching is one of the few jobs in which you not only can continue to keep in touch with your academic discipline, but in which you really have an obligation to do so, and to keep abreast of modern developments. If you are not a specialist and are a general class teacher you still find that you do have to go on learning, and many teachers take diplomas and certificates which improve their qualifications and which give them the opportunity of studying some aspects of child development.

Some teachers (on the whole more men than women) teach in the evenings at evening institutes and colleges of further education. This is another way in which teachers can pursue their own academic interests and hobbies and it gives them a chance of teaching adults. This makes a change but it is not necessarily more rewarding or more fun than teaching school children.

Many people find that a good way of going on with their own studies is to write while they are teaching; the most obvious form of writing to take up is textbook writing, and there are many men and some women who have made a great deal of money out of writing textbooks, as well as performing a very useful service and giving themselves great satisfaction.

14

THE TEACHER MECHANIZED?

ONE DAY I was told that we were to have a language laboratory, i.e. a collection of tape decks and microphone linked with a central control from which the teacher can monitor each pupil. This was something very exciting to contemplate but it also caused me furiously to think how we could best use such a heavy item of expenditure.

When I first heard of our laboratory there was very much less knowledge and experience of these aids to teaching than there is now, and the Mayfield modern language department had had no previous training in their use, except what they had done themselves by using tape recorders. One of the first difficulties was to decide where we could find a room both big enough and quiet enough to instal the new equipment. As, in spite of the size of the school, we have no spare rooms we had to adapt a room that was already being used by another department.

Then the staff and I tried to educate ourselves in the use of modern language teaching by means of language laboratories and we went on interesting visits to such places as the Shell language department and Ealing Technical College.

The proper use of aids such as language laboratories, which are very expensive, presents a great challenge to teachers, and there is certainly no fear that they will replace the teacher or make teaching easier. In fact, there is a 'Parkinsonian' element in all these developments because the machines cannot do the teaching themselves, and they have to be looked after. A new job that has developed is that of a technician or helper in a school where there are machines, television cameras, tape recorders and so on to be attended to.

There has recently been an enormous development in mechanical aids to teaching. Broadcast lessons have been known for many years now and were developed to a very high degree of efficiency and skill in the hey day of sound broadcasting. Recently television has been added to sound broadcasting, and now many schools have television sets which can be used by at least some of the classes, some of the time. The film, the film loop and the film strip all have different functions and can all be most usefully employed to supplement the teacher's work.

Recently the teaching machine has had a great deal of publicity, and in teaching situations outside school has undoubtedly had a very great success. The special feature of the teaching machine is that it is self-pacing, i.e. the pupil follows a programme and is prompted by the reaction of the machine to her answers to go on to the next stage of the particular subject being studied.

Of course, the criterion for assessing the teaching machine is not how efficient it is as a machine but how efficient is the programme or the text that it is using. Here is a challenge to teachers, and a new craft that teachers are taking up—the writing of programmes for teaching machines and also for programmed learning without a machine.

Teachers should not fear that teaching machines, language laboratories, television and so on will make them redundant. These are aids to teaching; they certainly cause the teacher to question her own skills, and her relationship with her pupils, but they should never destroy that relationship.

Modern medical practitioners have to understand and prescribe chemical medicines, but it is no good anybody thinking that these medicines do, in fact, replace the doctor, because it is the doctor who has to make the diagnosis and decide which variety of drug is suitable for which complaint and for which patient. In the same way teachers must understand these techniques of teaching and must decide when the machine is going to be an aid to her pupils, and then prescribe it and see that it is properly used.

The old image of a teacher, dowdily dressed, covered with chalk-dust and wearing a scowl, may live on in fiction and in entertainment, but in real life it is dead. The modern teacher is business-like, well-dressed and cheerful-looking. Not only is she competent with film projectors and tape recorders, but she also takes typewriters, duplicators and calculating machines in her stride. Where the local authority is generous and enlightened, she is supported by non-teaching staff who relieve her of some of the clerical work and technical preparation she has to do.

Chalk and talk remain among the essential basic tools you need to make the relationships which are at the heart of good teaching, but for you they will not be enough.

15

TEACHING GLADLY

'I COULDN'T TEACH, I haven't the patience,' I have heard people say. Is patience the most important quality that a teacher needs? I suppose it is of great value, though a degree of impatience is also necessary.

In the booklet on teaching as a career for graduates recently published by the Department of Education and Science, there is a chapter on the qualities required in teaching which begins in this way: 'What qualities then does the good teacher require? In any answer to this question, interest in children, patience, knowledge, inventiveness, understanding, wisdom, sympathy and humour would all find a place.'

Faced with such a formidable inventory, students might well doubt whether they could fill the bill, and indeed many people would think, 'Well, I haven't got all those things so I couldn't be a teacher.' But I wonder, if they really began to do a little self-assessment, whether they might not find that they had some at least of the qualities which are required in a teacher and whether the qualities which they are doubtful about, could not be expected to develop on the job?

A sense of humour is often listed as a desirable and even essential quality in a teacher. I am sure it is, as long as it is not exercised at the expense of the pupil. Shared laughter is a powerful aid to learning, but laughter 'at' can be a cruel deterrent. Every teacher must be aware of the difference between loud and excited laughter and that more gentle, chuckly kind of laughter which comes with happy understanding and appreciation of a joke or a funny situation.

Teachers must be pretty tough physically, although they have comparatively long holidays which compensate for the very considerable physical demands made during term time. A teacher must not be away from work if she can possibly avoid it. In many jobs a day's absence here and there simply means that work accumulates and that tackling it is postponed; no great harm is done.

A day's teaching timetable, though, cannot be postponed; the children are there and somebody has got to do something about them. Broken attendance on the part of a child has a very bad effect on her own development; the constant absence of a teacher has a most disturbing effect on the development of dozens of children and adds greatly to the work of her colleagues. So a teacher needs to be physically strong and to have some measure of stoicism.

At least nowadays people do not have to go into teaching when they really do not want to; there are plenty of other openings for women and this fact has undoubtedly raised the general standard of recruitment to the profession.

I can remember people who taught me and some whom I have had as colleagues, who ought never to have gone in for teaching at all; they simply did not seem to be able to get over to the pupils what it was all about. There was constant misunderstanding and often complete lack of communication, and this produced the worst kind of disorder in the minds of the children and in the results of the lesson. If no real communication has taken place, if no development of mind or personality has happened at all, then the day has been a lost one.

Of course, sometimes people say they do not want to go in for teaching, not because they do not think that they have the qualities that are necessary, but because they are afraid of not growing up themselves. I can think of instances when I have felt that a teacher of infants has remained rather juvenile and playful, even coy, in her conversation; when a prep school master does not seem to have grown in his interests beyond those of the boys, but these examples are not typical of the profession as a whole: moreover the same traits of behaviour, if not for the same reasons, can certainly be found in other professions.

Teachers of today are people who play a very full part in society outside school, and who would certainly not be able to cope with the job and with all its commitments beyond the classroom if they were not themselves mature people. Maturity is perhaps the most important quality that the teacher needs; after all judgements have constantly to be made and attitudes to other people need to be founded on a real maturity. Pettiness, childishness, jealousies, favouritism—all these things are marks of immaturity and must never appear in the behaviour and attitudes of a teacher.

I do not know whether awareness can be said to be a quality, but it is a very, very important thing for every teacher to be conscious, and to be sensitively aware, of the reactions of each pupil in the class.

In supervising the work of students or sometimes in visiting lessons, even those given by qualified teachers, I have seen many heartbreaking instances of the teacher not having registered what was behind the question asked or the answer given by a pupil; when a probing or a searching has been begun by the pupil and the teacher simply has not cottoned on. A most frustrating situation follows and the child begins to switch off and to give up trying.

This is one of the sad things that sometimes happens in our schools, and the teacher has a tremendous responsibility to see that her pupils' curiosity and awareness, excitement and interest in all sorts of things, whether they appear to be relevant or not to the lesson, are not squashed.

During thirty years of teaching I have worked in maintained schools, an independent school, and a university, and as I look back I think how wrong people are who think of teaching as a dull job. I can hardly ever remember being bored by my job. Nor have I been conscious of my work being repetitive, which is one of the things that people sometimes hold against teaching. 'How can you possibly bear to go on doing the same thing over and over again?' They say.

For me it hardly ever seems to have been the same thing. Your colleagues change, your pupils change, your ideas change, and of course you change your job from time to time; and you change yourself. But I think one of the reasons, perhaps the strongest reason, why you do not get bored in teaching is that it really is a creative job.

I have often found in discussing with people of similar educational backgrounds to my own, who are working perhaps in the civil service or in local government or in business, that they sometimes find it frustrating to be away from the coal face—from the actual people for whom the whole paraphernalia of the civil service and local government business is arranged.

Administration can be imaginative and often is, and it can be satisfying, but there is something about teaching, as I suppose there is about medicine and nursing, that gives you this constant awareness of being with people who are always changing, and who are constantly surprising you with their responses.

You cannot hope to see very clear results—at least not measurable results. But as Christopher Wren said '*Si monumentum requiris, circumspice*'. If you think of yourself as one of the many thousands of teachers each influencing, I suppose, an average of several hundred young people every year, you ought to feel some responsibility for the standards of society itself.

It has been said that you hear your teachers thirty years later for it is often long after they have left school that many people really begin to profit from the education they have received. Every teacher must have experienced that shock, sometimes of pride and happiness, when a former pupil quotes something that was said to her and which has been a great guide and strength to her in her adult life.

You can be equally shocked at the rather footling and silly things you said which are remembered and quoted against you, often I think with a certain amount of pleasant maliciousness! In any case these instances are reminders of the immense responsibility of the teacher.

I suppose really the test of a primary school teacher is what sort of secondary school pupil Mary makes. The success of a secondary teacher can be tested by the sort of employee, student, citizen, and parent, that Mary becomes. The power of a teacher is very considerable and should be recognised, because if wielded without awareness it can do harm to other personalities.

I have been constantly amazed at how individual teachers can encourage or inhibit an individual child; how a teacher can

integrate or disintegrate a class or a form or a tutor group; how
individual teachers can recognise and foster latent powers in
their pupils, or can kill them stone dead by lack of awareness.

Many young people say that when they go to work they want
to work with people. Well, the thing about teaching is that you
never get away from people—pupils, staff, parents, officials,
ordinary citizens. There is daily contact with most of these
groups and, of course, always with young people who are
constantly growing and changing.

A school, after all, never stays exactly the same. Each year a
considerable proportion of pupils leave and another group come
in, and those in the school are growing, in a secondary school
for example, from young boys and girls of eleven, who are
really still children, to mature young men and women of eighteen
or nineteen. So that the pupils themselves, apart from all the other
people that the teacher meets, are constantly changing and
growing and making different demands.

You have in teaching this fascinating mixture of permanence
and renewal. The staff, roughly speaking, stay permanent, but
their pupils are constantly being renewed, and, if they are good
teachers, so is what they teach.

As teachers we are part of the future, but we also have a share
in shaping this future by the way we hand on the wisdom of
the present and the past. Indeed the quality of the future is
determined in some measure by the interests that the teachers
stimulate, by the doors they open, by the standards they set,
by the ideals they strive for, by the attitudes they seek to establish.

APPENDIX

H.M. STATIONERY OFFICE, Kingsway, London, W.C.2. publishes a list of the Colleges of Education, List 172, price 1s. 6d. For more detailed information most schools and libraries have a copy of the Association of Teachers in Colleges and Departments of Education Handbook on *Training for Teaching*, while the Advisory Centre for Education has just published a Guide to Colleges of Education.

Information about students' grants can be obtained from the Local Education Authority or from the Department of Education and Science in Form 101, R.T.C. and particulars of teachers' salaries, the Burnham Scales, can be obtained from H.M. Stationery Office, Kingsway, London, W.C.2.

The following list of addresses may be helpful:—

THE UNIVERSITY CENTRAL COUNCIL ON ADMISSIONS,
29 Tavistock Square, London, W.C.1.

CENTRAL REGISTER AND CLEARING HOUSE (COLLEGES OF EDUCATION),
131 Gower Street, London, W.C.1.

NATIONAL UNION OF TEACHERS,
Hamilton House, Mapledon Place, London, W.C.1.

EDUCATIONAL INSTITUTE OF SCOTLAND,
46 Moray Place, Edinburgh, 3.

COLLEGE OF PRECEPTORS,
Bloomsbury Square, London,W.C.1.

JOINT COMMITTEE OF FOUR SECONDARY ASSOCIATIONS,
   The Association of Headmistresses
   The Incorporated Association of Headmasters
   The Association of Assistant Mistresses
   The Association of Assistant Masters
29 Gordon Square, London, W.C.1.

ADVISORY CENTRE FOR EDUCATION,
57 Russell Street, Cambridge.

DEPARTMENT OF EDUCATION AND SCIENCE,
Curzon Street, London, W.1.

SCOTTISH EDUCATION DEPARTMENT,
23 Ainslie Place, Edinburgh, 3.

MINISTRY OF EDUCATION FOR NORTHERN IRELAND,
Dundonald House, Upper Newtownards Road, Belfast, 4.

And for teaching overseas:—

NATIONAL COUNCIL FOR SUPPLY OF TEACHERS OVERSEAS,
Appointments Officer, Education, Ministry of Overseas
   Development, Eland House, Stag Place, London, S.W.1.

ENGLISH TEACHING REGISTER,
c/o Recruitment Division, British Council, 65 Davies Street,
   London, W.1.

OVERSEAS APPOINTMENTS BUREAU,
38 King Street, London, W.C.2.

CONFERENCE OF MISSIONARY SOCIETIES,
Edinburgh House, 2 Eaton Gate, London, S.W.1.

CENTRAL BUREAU FOR EDUCATIONAL VISITS AND EXCHANGES,
55a Duke Street, London, W.1.

VOLUNTARY SERVICE OVERSEAS,
3 Hanover Street, London, W.1.